W9-BRR-225

RELEASED *from* SHAME

Recovery for Adult Children of Dysfunctional Families

SANDRA D. WILSON

PEOPLE HELPER BOOKS,
GARY R. COLLINS, *series editor*

INTERVARSITY PRESS
DOWNERS GROVE, ILLINOIS 60515

© 1990 by Sandra D. Wilson

All rights reserved. No part of this book may be reproduced in any form without written permission from InterVarsity Press, P.O. Box 1400, Downers Grove, Illinois 60515.

InterVarsity Press is the book-publishing division of InterVarsity Christian Fellowship, a student movement active on campus at hundreds of universities, colleges and schools of nursing in the United States of America, and a member movement of the International Fellowship of Evangelical Students. For information about local and regional activities, write Public Relations Dept., InterVarsity Christian Fellowship, 6400 Schroeder Rd., P.O. Box 7895, Madison, WI 53707-7895.

All Scripture quotations, unless otherwise indicated, are from the Holy Bible, New International Version. Copyright © 1973, 1978, International Bible Society. Used by permission of Zondervan Bible Publishers.

ISBN 0-8308-1601-1

Printed in the United States of America ∞

Library of Congress Cataloging-in-Publication Data

Wilson, Sandra D., 1938-
   Released from shame: recovery for adult children of dysfunctional
families/by Sandra D. Wilson.
     p.   cm.—(People helper books)
   ISBN 0-8308-1601-1
   1. Adult children of dysfunctional families—United States—
Religious life. 2. Adult children of dysfunctional families—
United States—Pastoral counseling of. 3. Christian life—1960-
I. Title. II. Series.
BV4596.A274W54   1990
248.8'6—dc20   90-41846
                                CIP

13	12	11	10	9	8	7	6	5	4	3	2	1
99	98	97	96	95	94	93	92	91	90			

Bookstore

484

2/19/91

ACKNOWLEDGMENTS

Many individuals contributed to making this book a reality.

My friend and mentor Dr. Gary Collins first suggested the possibility.

*Don Stephenson, my editor at InterVarsity Press, kept me on course
once I began.*

*Senior pastor, Dr. Ray Dupont, and my other staff colleagues at Faith
Evangelical Free Church in Milford, Ohio, consistently upheld me with their
encouragements and prayers.*

*My children, Becky, Dave, and his wife, Dru, performed enthusiastic "cheerleading
drills" when I was weary of mind and body.*

*My wonderful husband, Garth, provided unfailing love and assurances of his
confidence in me and the ministry to which God has called me.*

*And scores of Christian brothers and sisters shared their struggles and pain-bought
victories as, together, we learn to walk in God's truth.*

My deepest gratitude goes to all of you.

*Finally, and above all, with thanksgiving and inexpressible joy I dedicate this book to
the glory of God, the only true father I have ever known.*

82844

Introduction

This book is for and about adult children from dysfunctional families. The words *adult children* signify something more than offspring over the age of eighteen. The term might even refer to you. If you identify with the term *adult child*, it's probably because you often feel as if a needy child is alive (and not too well) inside your adult body.

Families become dysfunctional, unhealthy and pain-filled because one or both parents are impaired. The impairment could stem from alcoholism, other drug abuse or a mental or emotional disturbance, such as chronic rage or depression. Parents who have impairments often abuse their children emotionally, sexually and/or physically. And, of course, these abuses have long-range, far-reaching effects.

Offspring of impaired parents often have bookshelves that sag under the weight of accumulated self-help guides. (You should see *my* collection!) If you grew up in what is commonly called a dysfunctional family, as I did, you might already have leafed through the scores of self-help books available these days. And if you are a Christian you probably rejoice with me that there is much available about adult child issues from a Christian perspective. So, do you really need another adult child book?

Let me help you decide. Before you spend your time reading this book, why not take a brief quiz to determine if it's right for you.

1. When you hear the phrase, "There's no place like home," do you:
   a. smile
   b. wince
   c. gag
   d. panic

If you answered either *b, c* or *d,* this book is for you.

2. Have you memorized all the words to "Jesus Loves Me This I Know" but seriously suspect you might have fallen through the cracks?

3. Do you often feel like the only caterpillar in a world full of butterflies?

If thoughts of home don't make you smile, and if you answered yes to the other questions, this book could help you—especially if you answered yes to the last question. I'm thinking about someone like you as I write. That sense of being the only caterpillar in a butterfly world captures the feeling of shame that binds millions of adults to painful pasts and the horrors of a hopeless future.

Shame is a sense of being uniquely and hopelessly flawed. Shame leaves a person feeling different from and less valuable than other human beings.

Shame is different from guilt. Guilt tells me that I made a mistake. Shame shouts that I AM a mistake. If my behavior is faulty, I can correct it and change. If my very *being* is flawed, I am without hope for change.

This book is about the legacy of lies and shame inherited by adult children from dysfunctional families. It is also about the life-transforming power of truth and the hope for change it brings. As adult children, we might be living our lives based on choices we made as confused, often abused, children in family systems committed to denying the truth. Change follows new and better choices, and we need truth to recognize those choices.

Here is one crucial kernal of truth: We do not live in a butterfly world. Therefore, this book does not contain a formula to make you perfect. You are a caterpillar, and so am I. Just as caterpillars are in metamorphosis, we are "in-process people." That is what we are intended to be. That is what we will always be.

Throughout our personal metamorphoses, God sees us as complete and perfect if we are Christians. And God is neither surprised nor disappointed that we are not completely perfected in our current lives on earth. God loves us so much that he *accepts* us right where we are. But he loves us too much to *leave* us right where we are.

God has a plan for us caterpillar Christians, and he calls it transformation (from the Greek word *metamorpheo*). According to Romans 12:2, this transformation is the result of a lifelong process of mind renewal. The book before you is intended to be one part of your personal metamorphosis.

Certainly it has been part of mine! I am writing not from a "holier than thou" or even necessarily a "healthier than thou" stance. I openly acknowledge that I am a recovering perfectionist and approval addict. And I confess that one of my goals is to stay "one valley ahead" of my clients in this journey of recovery and transformation. Sometimes I make it. Sometimes I'm not so sure.

Let me tell you what you'll find in the following pages. In chapter one, I tell you something about myself and why I understand adult children and our shame symptoms. Chapters two through six describe shame and its origins in various types of dysfunctional families. Chapter seven elaborates the causes of shame and the hope for change.

In the remaining chapters, I address aspects of adult children's personal and interpersonal lives that are most often bound by shame. And I suggest new choices that lead to change, because understanding our past pain and present problems is not enough. We must use our increased understanding to guide our new choices. Without new choices, we remain stuck going around and around in the old, familiar, painful grooves.

Since it is often difficult to recognize these painful patterns, I encourage you to begin each reading time by praying for insight and understanding from God. James 1:5 promises wisdom from God to those who seek it. And Psalm 51:6 assures you that God not only wants you to be truthful about your inner person, but that he will give you wisdom in the parts hidden from your awareness.

Believe me, you can trust God's timing. He won't hit you with more than you and he can handle together. I know that's true from my own life and from the lives of those I counsel. And remember, you now have resources that you did not have as a child. You can find a friend, pastor, counselor, group or other human supporters to help by listening, believing, comforting and/or confronting you with truth.

Keep a journal of your thoughts and feelings as you read. Some people like to devote time to journal-keeping when they read the Bible and pray. They often write about how the Scripture they read applies to their transformation processes. Other people use their journals to pour out painful emotions they want to share with God.

You can also use your journal to enhance the self-examination opportunities offered in the "Time Out" and "Personal Reflection" sections of this book. Even if you have no intention of keeping a personal journal, please take a few moments to consider the questions and issues raised in these special sections of each chapter.

Finally, here are some thoughts for those of you who feel vaguely guilty about reading a counseling book. Beyond a doubt, God's Word contains all the principles we need to live a life that glorifies him. But let's not limit God when it comes to the methods he uses to apply biblical principles in our lives. Jesus chose human helpers to unbind Lazarus after God raised him from the dead. Clearly, Jesus did not need help! Today God often heals physical wounds through physicians and other human instruments. Similarly, he often heals *emotional* wounds through counselors and/or books that apply scriptural truths.

This book focuses on the scriptural truth that each of us is an imperfect, mistake-making, sinful "caterpillar" who lives in a world of imperfect, mistake-making, sinful "caterpillars." Yet, if you are a Christian, Scripture declares that you are in the process of being transformed (metamorphosed) more and more into Christ's likeness. This is God's plan and purpose for us. And he promises to complete this "good work" he has begun. (See Romans 8:29 and Philippians 1:6.)

Dear fellow caterpillar, I am praying that God will use this book as a meaningful part of your ongoing personal metamorphosis.

1
My Story: "Half a Loaf"

I *was almost an abortion.*

And I would have been, had my earthly father's plans succeeded. Obviously, my heavenly Father had other plans, and my mother was on God's side. I have never met, seen or viewed a photograph of my biological father. Everything I know about him comes from my mother. She describes him as having a brilliant intellect, a charismatic personality and a disturbed mind.

Mother believes that my father married her because she had a small sum of money and planned to move from her native Massachusetts (where they met) to Arizona. After their marriage, Mother learned that my father, who was twelve years her senior, had abandoned his wife and four children in New York state. He needed to get away from New England and was eager to settle in Phoenix.

My father was furious when he learned that Mother was pregnant.

After she refused to get an abortion, my father arranged for one. However, she managed to thwart his plans, "with God's guidance," as Mother recalls. My father tried to kill Mother three times once she was pregnant, but further danger was averted when my father's past mail fraud caught up with him. When I was born, my parents were divorced, and my father was in a federal prison.

I started life in a single-parent household long before it was fashionable.

Another Father

My mother met and married my stepfather when I was almost two years old. A truck driver, he had been in an accident which put him in the hospital. Mother had been his physical therapist. My stepfather had no access to liquor in the hospital, so Mother didn't learn that he was an alcoholic until after their brief courtship and marriage.

During the World War 2 years, my stepfather "volunteered" for the army in lieu of going to prison for parole violations of alcohol-related violence. Mother and I lived with a family who cared for me while Mother worked. Feeling guilty that she had deprived me of a "normal" father, Mother began teaching me when I was very young that God was my *heavenly* Father who would always love me.

The Alcoholic Years

When I was seven, my stepfather rejoined the family, and we moved into the small home Mother bought with her wartime savings. The next two years were a blur of arguments between my parents. Most of the quarrels were about my stepfather's drunken behavior and financial entanglements. During this time, my mother threatened to divorce him if he didn't stop drinking, so he joined Alcoholics Anonymous to placate her. She later learned that he continued to drink when away on trucking runs.

Two memories stand out during those years. First, I dimly remember going with my stepfather on a few short trips in his truck. I longed for his attention and love, yet I remember feeling vaguely unsafe.

The other memory concerns a *clearly* unsafe situation in which I was molested by a stranger. Like most frightened little girls, I felt dirty and somehow to blame. And like most frightened little girls, I never told anyone.

Gaining a Brother

My mother deliberately got pregnant with my brother, Ron, even though she knew her marriage was crumbling. During the pregnancy, my stepfather's drinking and violence escalated. I remember that my mother and I spent the night with friends on several occasions because Mother was afraid of my stepfather's alcoholic rages.

By that time, I knew my stepfather had a drinking problem. Mother spoke of it openly. I remember worrying about my mother and feeling somehow responsible to make her happy. Like the overly responsible "hero" I was becoming, I tried to be a perfect child so I wouldn't add to Mother's burdens. I sensed that my survival depended on keeping Mother from collapsing under the weight of her full-time physical therapy practice and her deteriorating marriage. If something happened to her, I would be left with only my alcoholic stepfather. That was a terrifying thought.

My brother was born four months before my tenth birthday, and I was thrilled! I adored Ron and zealously undertook the big-sister role.

Losing a Father

The marriage survived four years after Ron's birth. What a kaleidoscope of jumbled memory fragments those years are for me. When I was ten, my mother finally told me that my stepfather was not my "real" biological father. I remember feeling shock, confusion, relief and sadness.

Three terrifying memories tower above all others from the years when I was ten to thirteen. First, I remember the night my mother went out with my stepfather to a bar, leaving me to baby-sit with Ron. When they returned, Mother kissed me, and I could smell alcohol on her breath. I was paralyzed with fear! My Rock of Gibraltar was crumbling, and my mind exploded with questions. What would I do if she began drinking too? How could I take care of myself and my baby brother? Fortunately, that evening was the exception, not the rule.

Second, I remember one Friday evening when my stepfather was violently drunk. He phoned from a bar declaring his intention to kill Mother when he came home. We locked all the doors and waited. Ron was already sleeping peacefully in his crib when his father appeared. My stepfather smashed his hand through the glass portion of the kitchen door to unlock it, while Mother and I barricaded ourselves in my bedroom. When my stepfather discovered that, he got a hammer and began bashing in my bedroom door. Mother and I crawled out my window onto the front porch and fled to the next-door neighbors. Later she called the police.

I remember the terror of that escape. And I remember feeling humiliated by having a police car, its lights flashing wildly, parked in front of our house. That evening ended with my stepfather sleeping on the living room sofa while Mother and I sought refuge with neighbors.

The next morning, I had to go in the house to get my gym shorts because I was scheduled to run in a seventh-grade track meet. Blood and vomit were splattered around the living room where my stepfather was still sprawled on the sofa. He had cut his hand smashing the glass in the kitchen door. And he concluded his homicide attempt by throwing up all over himself, the sofa and the carpet.

I don't remember much about my track meet that day.

The final towering memory from those years lay unclaimed in my mind for decades. I remembered it suddenly and clearly about eight years ago as I read about abuse in alcoholic families.

On a vacation trip to Massachusetts the summer I turned eleven, we stopped in Missouri to visit my stepfather's sister and her husband. For some reason I've never understood, my mother, stepfather and stepaunt left me and my brother in the care of my stepuncle one evening. While they were away, the man molested me. I remember him sitting on the couch where I was supposed to be asleep. He fondled my genitals and my budding breasts as I lay frozen by fear, hoping he would think I was sleeping. It seemed he was there forever before he finally stopped. Eventually I went to sleep that night, and so did the memory. It slumbered safely out of my awareness for more than thirty years.

Like most adult children from dysfunctional families, I have "forgotten" a lot of traumatic experiences from my childhood. For instance, my mother recently asked me if I remember the evening my intoxicated, angry stepfather locked her, Ron and me out of the house. (I don't.) She pounded on the door, begging him to let us in, but he refused. Carrying Ron, who was still an infant, Mother walked with me to a nearby service station to phone my stepfather. Having no success, we walked back home and slept in the family car that night. Fortunately, it was summer.

My mother and stepfather were divorced a few days before my graduation from eighth grade. I remember telling my small circle of friends that the divorce was "the best graduation present I could ever have."

A Heavenly Father

The year before the divorce, my mother began attending a Baptist church in Phoenix. She had abandoned her Catholic heritage as a girl but had continued to love God and to sense his love for her. Within months of my mother's conversion and baptism, I too became a Christian and began to love the Bible and to hunger for its wisdom. My church friends became a caring family, and I learned to love my heavenly Father more and more.

Married . . . with Baggage

I met my future husband, Garth, when I was a freshman at Arizona State University, majoring in psychology. His folks readily accepted me because I was a Christian; I became the daughter they'd never had. My mother liked Garth because he was strong and sensible—not at all like the "strays," as she called them, that I usually brought home.

Garth and I were married on April 3, 1958, during spring break of my sophomore and his senior year. I was nineteen, and he was five days short of twenty-one.

Have you ever heard a couple described as "married . . . with children"? Well, we were *married . . . with baggage.* (The children came a few years later.) From what I have already told you about my childhood, you can picture the size and shape of *my* baggage.

Garth had his own uniquely designed emotional baggage. His father had a drinking problem throughout the first ten years of Garth's life. And even when Mr. Wilson overcame his alcoholism, his workaholism continued. Garth remembers his father as kind but distant and emotionally unavailable, and his mother as loving but preoccupied with her husband's alcoholism and her other son's illnesses.

Garth was a bright, independent kid who used his athletic ability to keep busy away from the house. His mother became a Christian when she was pregnant with Garth, and she always took her sons to church even though her husband never went. Garth became a Christian when he was eight, but spiritual growth took a back seat to sports.

Just after our marriage, a pattern emerged: Garth expressed his anger through hostility and rage while I repressed my anger through depression and denial. Garth soon replicated his father's workaholic approach to life, while I buried myself in motherhood and self-righteous "sanctified workaholism" at church.

Dave was born in 1960, and Becky followed two and a half years later. Both were very wanted and very loved. And both were born into a second-generation dysfunctional family. Dave and Becky remember spending a lot of time in church nurseries because their mom was using Baptistic busyness to numb her personal pain. For several years Garth refused to attend church at all, but that didn't decrease my evangelical hyperactivity!

We relocated several times during those years as Garth climbed the corporate ladder. Meanwhile, my chronic, mild depression erupted into a deep, clinical depression. In many ways my body expressed the emotional pain I felt. Finally, our family physician told me to get counseling because I had numerous depression-related and stress-attributed health problems.

The subsequent six months of psychotherapy began my ongoing

emotional mending process. As I examined my past, I faced my anger and my need to grieve childhood losses. God also supplied a spiritually mature Christian woman to provide the biblical perspective missing in my therapy. Marie helped me face my need to forgive myself as well as my parents and others.

By the time the family moved to Cincinnati in 1972, I was much less depressed. However, Garth and I still had not addressed the unhealthy aspects of our relationship. But we both stayed absorbed in other areas of our lives: work and children for him, and children and leading Bible studies for me.

My love for studying and teaching Scripture had grown during the years, and I was leading two Bible studies a week. My teaching style was always heavy on personal application. And as I began to discuss my depression and God's work in my life, more and more women in the study began coming to me for informal counseling.

About that time, I attended a series of classes on what was called *biblical counseling*. I was thrilled to learn that there was a name for what I had been doing and that there were actually Christian mental-health professionals doing *formally* what I had been doing *informally*. I devoured *How to Be a People Helper* by Gary Collins and Larry Crabb's *Effective Biblical Counseling*. God used those books, the series of classes, my love for the practical application of Scripture, insights from my painful past and my desire to serve him to call me into a ministry of Christian counseling.

Late Blooming

At forty-one, I returned to college to finish my undergraduate degree in psychology. Dave was at the University of California on a swimming scholarship. Becky was a junior in high school, a top student and co-captain of the basketball and swimming teams. I managed to carry a heavy course load and keep my grades up without missing any of her activities. (Now *that's* perfectionistic pleasing and performing!)

After Becky left to attend Texas Christian University, I started on my master's program. And when I finished that, at the age of forty-four, I began my first full-time job.

I was a classic "late bloomer." *But no one warned me about the thorns.* My increased sense of self-sufficiency fueled the flames of repressed anger at Garth. My spiritual life was at low tide, and I thought that divorcing Garth was my only chance for fulfillment. He was shocked by my request for a separation, and he began to pray that God would save our marriage. Garth sought Christian counseling, confessed his unloving and angry behavior and promised to continue relying on God to change. Meanwhile, God broke through my anger and spiritual apathy to convince me that I was on a dangerously self-destructive path. I agreed to go with Garth for counseling to rebuild our marriage.

Even now, seven years later, I am blinking back tears as I write about that incredibly painful place in our lives. I am overwhelmed with God's grace and power. He gave me the courage to confront my own sin and selfishness and my need to change. He enabled me to trust him even when I couldn't trust Garth to keep his promises. And God empowered Garth to make enormous changes in his attitudes and actions. When the children were home for Christmas that year, even *they* noticed that their dad was much kinder and less angry.

That crisis in our marriage marked a turning point in our lives and our relationship. Do we ever have problems anymore? Of course we do, because we're still selfish sinners. But I can say truthfully that our marriage is being transformed and we have never been more in love.

Still in Process

During the past few years, I have become more aware of my adult child issues. I had read extensively on the subject of adult children of alcoholics even before my research and writing.[1] I also attend and conduct workshops, seminars and support groups for adult children from dysfunctional families. Most important, I continue to apply the truths of God's Word to my life. Nevertheless, I have not "arrived." I am still in process, and sometimes that is *painfully* obvious, as you will discover in subsequent chapters. The truth is, I am a caterpillar just like you. I am still in the process of being transformed by the renewing of my mind. I *always* will be. God understands that, and that's just fine with both of us.

Daily I am amazed by my gracious, loving Lord. My husband is God's love-gift to me. Becky and Dave (and Dave's bride, Dru) love the Lord, and I would choose them for friends even if they were not relatives. My brother and I have become cherished friends as well as family. My mother and I can talk openly about the pain of her past and mine, and we give God glory in it all. Additionally, God has opened doors for me to teach at one of America's finest seminaries, direct a church-based counseling program, and write and speak about his power to redeem pain and transform lives.

Increasingly, I am learning to accept my human limitations. I am continuing to recover from my approval addiction and perfectionism, without relinquishing my deep commitment to excellence. Nevertheless, at times I resort to my perfectionistic pleasing and performing, and then berate myself for not being perfectly recovered from perfectionism! See what I mean about an ongoing, lifelong process?

Half a Loaf

In Matthew 7:9, Jesus implied that fathers don't ordinarily give their children stones when asked for bread. I've heard that loaves of bread in Jesus' day were shaped like smooth, round stones, so the imagery was particularly potent to his audience.

Have you ever heard the expression, "half a loaf is better than none"? I feel as if I received "half a loaf" as a child. My mother gave me the nurturing "bread" of her sincere love, while my father gave me the "stone" of complete rejection and abandonment. I am reminded of my "half a loaf" every time I need to give my medical history and am unable to answer questions about my paternal heredity.

Half a loaf was my legacy, and it *is* better than none. I know that some of you received stones from *both* parents when you asked for bread. My heart aches for you. What are we to do if we received half a loaf—or none at all?

I pondered that question as I prayed and read the Bible a few months ago. I was thinking of the many incest survivors I counsel who received from their parents hideous, heavy stones in place of tender, nurturing bread. And I also thought about my own half a loaf. The Holy Spirit led me to read Deuteronomy 8:3, where Moses says of Jehovah God, "He humbled you, causing you to hunger and then feeding you with manna, which neither you nor your fathers had known, to teach you that man does not live on bread alone but on every word that comes from the mouth of the LORD." God used that verse to say:

Sandy, I lovingly and sovereignly allowed everything in your past that left you hungering for the approval of a father figure in your life.[2] I understand your pain and vulnerability in that area. I want to teach you that even if you *had* had two well-adjusted and extremely godly parents, that would not have been enough to satisfy the deep hunger of your soul. You will truly live and be fulfilled (literally *filled-full*) only as you continue to receive the bread from heaven, Jesus Christ, God's living Word and Scripture, God's written Word.

That was God's special message to this half-a-loaf child. I believe it is his message to all his children who feel like caterpillars in a butterfly world.

That's my story. Now let's look at yours. Each of our stories has been penned, in part, by our families.

Like me, many of you are from dysfunctional families. Each dysfunctional family is unique. Yet they all have a common denominator: denial of truth and bondage to shame. If you want to escape that legacy of lies and shame, you must commit to the transforming metamorphosis of mind renewal. And to move forward in your personal metamorphosis, you need to begin by understanding the dynamics of shame and then looking honestly at your past.

You can begin in chapter two.

2
Understanding Shame and Stumbling

*A*ll *my life, I've felt as though I have to work twice as hard to be half* as good as other people. But no matter how hard I try, I just never feel like I measure up or belong. Does this make any sense?"

The beautiful, intelligent Christian woman in my office made a lot of sense—especially when you consider that she was raised in an abusive family where her father violated her body and her mother assaulted her mind and soul.

Shame is a strong sense of being uniquely and hopelessly different and less than other human beings. When you experience shame, you feel isolated and alienated from others. It is as if you are standing alone on one side of a broken bridge while everyone else in the world stares at you from the other side.[1] Shame symptoms include beliefs, emotions and behaviors that display the underlying pain that comes from seeing ourselves as eternally separated from others.

In this chapter we will take a closer look at shame and examine the components that can contribute to symptoms of shame.

Shame can have three underlying components: the physical component in *biological shame;* the spiritual component in what I call *biblical shame;* and the psychological component in what I call *binding shame.*

Biological Shame

Biological shame is a child's time-limited, natural response to the observable differences between children and grown-ups.

As a child, you *were* physically and intellectually different and less than your parents and other adults. On some level of awareness you might have believed that your condition was unique and hopeless. And you might have assumed you were condemned to spend your entire existence *never* knowing how to solve the mysteries of mud, Monopoly or multiplication.

However, you already have observed that the basis of biological shame is transitory. The solution to the personal distress of biological shame is simple: aging. And at this point in your life, you might be taller, stronger and more highly skilled and/or educated than the very adults you once perceived as giant geniuses.

In the normal course of things, children outgrow the basis for biological shame. So how could it contribute to a sense of shame? The answer lies in the difference between functional and dysfunctional families. Functional families are committed to truth—including truth about human development. But dysfunctional families are centered on distortion and denial of truth.

Which of the following types of statements did you hear when you were a child? Your answer will serve as a clue about the level of family dysfunction in your childhood.

☐ "Why can't you keep up with me, Slow Poke? I haven't got all day." (Mother to three-year-old.)

☐ "You look like you're running to stay up with Mommy. My legs are longer than yours because I'm grown up, so I'd better slow down a little. I remember how hard it was for me to stay up with my mommy and daddy." (Mother to three-year-old.)

☐ "Now look what you did, you clumsy kid. What's the matter with you?" (Father to six-year-old who spilled milk.)

☐ "Oops, there goes the milk. I'll get a couple of paper towels, and you can have that cleaned up in just a minute. I'll help too. You know what? I think I filled that glass a little too full for you." (Father to six-year-old who spilled milk.)

You get the idea. Children naturally walk more slowly and are less coordinated than adults. These developmental deficits disappear in time, and they need not be a source of shame. They won't be if parents understand and consistently adapt their expectations to the truth about child development as the parents in the second and fourth statements did.

But some parents have unrealistic developmental expectations of a child, and then they shame their child for not fulfilling them. This is true of intellectual and skill development as well as of physical development.

If you were expected automatically to possess some information or master a skill you had never been taught, that enlarged your foundation of biological shame. I know of an eight-year-old daughter shamed for not understanding how to follow a recipe and a ten-year-old son shamed for not trimming hedges correctly. No one had taken the time to show them how to do the assigned tasks, but both were expected to perform perfectly.

The time and the emotional energy needed to understand and teach children are scarce commodities in dysfunctional homes. Did you notice that the second and fourth statements are longer than the first and third? Clearly, shaming a child's limited skill and knowledge is less time consuming than responding with understanding and patience.

From my perspective, there is no need for biological shame to contribute to shame in adults. Unless a developmental handicap intervenes, children will one day find themselves on the adult side of that bridge they once perceived as uncrossable. (Perhaps children are so delighted and fascinated when they first notice other children because they are

relieved to know there are some *other* short-legged, "clumsy" little beings in the world.)

But even if we outgrow a *biological* basis for shame, we still face two
others. One of these is biblical shame.

Biblical Shame

Biblical shame is an appropriate, healthy response when we acknowledge that we are different and less than God made us and that we are
separated from him by our sin. Although we bear the image of God,
sin radically altered our fundamental natures. Sin separates us from
ourselves as originally created. Sin separates us from our original Creator.

Scripture is full of statements about the differences between God and
human beings. Perhaps the summary statement is Isaiah 55:8: " 'For my
thoughts are not your thoughts, neither are your ways my ways,' declares the LORD." Now *there* is a sanctified understatement if I ever
heard one!

We can respond to our unbearable sense of separation from God in
one of three ways. First, we can deny the separation. This is what
secular humanists do by eliminating God and elevating human beings
to a level of unlimited potential. New Age adherents of Eastern mys-
ticism achieve the same end by ignoring the gulf between the natures
of God and human beings with declarations that they *are* God.

There is another group of people who do not deny their sin natures,
but they deny that God has provided a trustworthy "bridge" over the
chasm of separating sin. Whereas the first group says, "I am so good
I am innately united with God," the second says, "I am so bad I am
eternally alienated from God." The first see themselves without need;
the second see themselves without hope.

In contrast to those who choose to refuse a bridge to God, millions
have accepted God's perfect solution to the problem of being separated
from him. They have taken the only bridge that leads from darkness
to the light where God dwells and reigns.

That bridge is Jesus, who, though sinless himself, paid the penalty for our sin by dying on a cross in our place.

In John 14:6, Jesus tells his followers that he is truth and life and the only way (or bridge) to get to God. So the good news is that although we have need of a bridge because of our sin, we have the offer of a bridge because of God's love and grace. We will *always* be different and less than God. But when we accept his gift of grace through Jesus, we will no longer be alienated from him.

Both biological and biblical shame are based on the truth of a "different-and-less-than" status. In biological shame, that difference is in the developmental capacities of children as compared with adults. With biblical shame, the difference is in the essential nature of God in contrast to that of human beings. The solution to biological shame is *growth*. The solution to biblical shame is *grace*.

If we are now adult Christians, neither biological nor biblical shame need to contribute to our feelings of shame. However, this doesn't mean that Christian adults never struggle with shame.

Binding Shame

Neither grace nor growth automatically eliminate the third category, *binding shame*. Binding shame is rooted in childhood experiences in the family and in children's limited capacity to accurately interpret them.[2] To understand the power of these family experiences, we must understand how children can be "caused to stumble."

Cause 1: Parental Power to Cause "Stumbling"

Have you ever noticed that some children seem to go virtually skipping and giggling into adulthood on smooth, straight highways headed right into the open arms of God and success? Meanwhile, others are bruised and bloodied from scrambling over and around obstacles cluttering their twisted paths to personal and spiritual despair. What makes the difference?

They all share the same sin nature (see Romans 3:23), and ". . . God does not show favoritism . . . ," (see Acts 10:34) so that can't explain the differences. These persons are unique in their genetic endowments and in the choices they have made, it's true. But Jesus offers an explanation that transcends individual differences by looking *beyond* genetic endowment and *behind* personal choices.

Jesus clearly taught that children can be caused to stumble into sin. "Whoever causes one of these little ones who believe in Me to stumble, it is better for him that a heavy millstone be hung around his neck, and that he be drowned in the depth of the sea." (Matthew 18:6 NASB)

The word translated *stumble* in one Bible translation (and *sin* in others) paints a word picture of what children can be caused to do.[3] Parents and other adults can put obstacles of false teachings in children's paths. Because they believe these lies are truth and act on them, the children might experience disastrous personal and spiritual consequences.

In verse seven, Jesus issued a strong warning to those who *cause* the stumbling, not to the children who stumble. Apparently, children can be caused to stumble into hurtful, sinful patterns of living in ways that adults cannot. Perhaps the difference has something to do with choices.

Clearly, children don't have the same choices adults have. If you grew up in an English-speaking family you could not suddenly choose to speak Italian because you didn't like the sound of English. You knew no alternative language. You had no choice but to speak the language spoken by your family. And that language included the thought patterns behind the words. If you didn't have an alternative, you didn't really make a choice.

Similarly, children have no choices about what to accept as truth because they have only their parents' views of reality. And the parents' degree of commitment to truth is the most significant discriminator between functional and dysfunctional families.

The more significantly impaired parents are, for example, by alcoholism rather than by workaholism, the greater the need to distort reality to deny the impairment and its impact on the family. In effect, each family lives by its own unique ratio of truth to denial which determines the level of family functioning.

Figure 2-1 is a visual representation of this concept.

Family Functioning, Parental Impairment and the Truth-Denial Ratio

Consistent Denial of Truth		Consistent Display of Truth

|⊢————————————————⊦————————————————⊣|

Impaired and Consistently Inadequate Parenting		Imperfect but Consistently Adequate Parenting
EXTREMELY DYSFUNCTIONAL		**EXTREMELY FUNCTIONAL**

Figure 2-1.

Even on the extremely *dysfunctional* side of this continuum, there is neither *total* denial of truth nor *totally* inadequate parenting. Conversely, on the extremely *functional* end, parents do not *perfectly* display truth or *perfectly* fulfill their parenting tasks.

Parents display or deny truth by their words, attitudes and actions. Children inevitably believe that every parental frown or phrase, smile or syllable accurately reflects reality. This is the bedrock of binding shame. Parents and parental substitutes are the sole interpreters of reality to young children. Therefore their verbal and nonverbal statements are impressed like handprints in the wet cement of their children's minds.

Unrealistic is not found in the dictionary of childhood. Without inborn, accurate views of reality, young children are unable to distinguish realistic from unrealistic parental expectations. Young minds can not grasp the concept of parents thrusting on children's shoulders the unrealistic expectations that—decades before—had been thrust on them. Children have no way of understanding that when their parents withheld affirmation or inflicted abuse it revealed something sadly missing within the *parents* rather than something hopelessly flawed within the *children*.

If you were raised in a dysfunctional family, you were "caused to stumble." Unrealistic expectations and/or abusive treatment taught you the lies that you are the kind of child who deserves disrespectful and/or dehumanizing treatment, that parents can do anything they want to you, and that God doesn't care. And the more extreme the level of inadequate parenting, actual abuse and distortion of reality, the deeper is your sense of being innately different and deficient.

Clearly, a parent's power to cause stumbling plants the seeds of binding shame in the mind of a child. Yet, the child's limited reasoning ability plays a part in the growth of binding shame.

Cause 2: Children's Magical Thinking

All young children see themselves as the centers of the universe who possess awesome, unlimited powers to cause events. This is sometimes called magical thinking, and it translates into a kind of fairy-tale logic which teaches children that good things happen to good people and bad things happen to bad people. This has devastating results for children in dysfunctional families.

If you are from one of these families, you concluded at a very early age that the abuse was your fault because you believed that you caused *everything*. In a healthy family you naturally outgrow magical thinking as you bump against the firm limitations of your personal power. But in unhealthy families, magical thinking is reinforced if you're told that you caused Dad's drinking, Mom's tirades or even your own abuse.

Can you see how magical thinking could merge with your primitive awareness that you were a hopeless disappointment to your parents because you weren't perfect? Your conclusion was that if you were a different, acceptable, "good" (meaning perfect) child, you would not be abused. You assumed you were being treated in the manner you deserved. (That's one reason why adults who are abused as children repeatedly get into abusive relationships throughout their lives. On some deep level, they believe that those are the only kinds of relationships they deserve.)

Binding shame flourishes as parents sow their unrealistic developmental demands and other abuses in the soil of magical thinking. But there is a third element. In a paradoxical way, binding shame provides children with an illusion of protective power.

Cause 3: Need for Protective Illusions

Regardless of how painful it was to believe that you were so bad you caused your "perfectly nice parents" to severely or subtly abuse you, there is something worse.

Experts who worked with delinquent children from extremely dysfunctional and abusive homes were struck by:

the refusal of these children to characterize their parents as bad and by the intensity of their devotion to mothers and fathers who were both neglectful and abusive. . . . Children who would not accuse the worst parents of bad behavior would easily accuse themselves of being bad children.[4]

It is terrifying to acknowledge that your parents made their own bad choices about how to treat you and that you were utterly powerless to control them. A young child's unconscious reasoning probably goes like this: "If I can cause something (for example, abuse) then I can make it happen or not happen." This provides an illusion of control for children (and often for adults) and is less frightening than the truth.

Time Out

Take a moment right now to look at a picture of yourself when you were five or six years old. Notice how small, perhaps fragile, you look. Now ask yourself, what could you have done to defend yourself against *anything* your parents might have chosen to do to you?

If that question causes you to feel anxious as an adult, just imagine how overwhelmingly terrifying it would be to a child. Is it any wonder children in dysfunctional families cling to the illusion of control by seeing themselves as so different and less worthy than other children that they are "bad" enough to deserve neglect and/or abuse?

The reality is that children are totally vulnerable to the whims of imperfect and impaired adults. Therefore, children feel safer being the "bad" ones rather than facing the terror of acknowledging that their parents could choose to be "bad" no matter what the children did or didn't do.

This illusory protection exacts a costly toll as children from dysfunctional families stumble into adulthood bearing the wounds of binding shame.

Personal Reflection

☐ The Bible says a lot about stumbling. For example, Psalm 56:13 says: "For you have delivered me from death and my feet from stumbling, that I may walk before God in the light of life." Do you see evidence of this in your life?

☐ What might God use to light your path so you could identify obstacles over which you have stumbled in the past and over which you might continue to stumble? (See Psalm 119:105 for a hint.)

☐ What are some *specific* ways you could cooperate with God's plan to use that source of illumination on *your* path?

☐ Jude 23 (NASB) refers to God as, "Him who is able to keep you from stumbling, and to make you stand in the presence of His glory blameless with great joy." Take a moment to thank God for this promise.

Looking Ahead

You might have been caused to stumble off a four-inch curb and barely "skin" your knee. Or, you might have been caused to stumble off a forty-foot cliff which has left you broken, bruised and bleeding from deep, gaping wounds.

Whether we find ourselves lying by a small curb or a great cliff (or by something in between) you or I might ask "how did I get here?" We will consider the answer in chapters three through seven.

3
Shame in Dysfunctional Families

While attending a conference recently, I was taking a walk on a Scottsdale, Arizona, road when a couple stopped me for directions. The man greeted me in a lilting British accent and then anxiously thrust a hotel brochure map at me, asking how to get to Scottsdale's Old Town shopping area.

I explained that Old Town was behind us to the south, and since they were already several miles north of Scottsdale, they were heading further away from their destination. The couple exchanged perplexed looks as I noticed the name of their hotel. Like mine, their hotel was located north of Scottsdale, so to reach their goal they should have headed south that morning. When they realized their mistake, they were embarrassed for not knowing where they started in relationship to their desired destination.

I know many Christian adults raised in dysfunctional families who are like that confused but well-meaning couple. They want to make new choices, but they lack a context for change. You might be one of them.

The British couple's point of origin was their hotel north of Scottsdale. Yours is a combination of your past experiences, most of which involved your family. No matter how much you might desire it, you cannot cut yourself off from the past and its influences on you. Who you are today and how you relate to God and others is due, in part, to your past experiences. Those experiences were formed uniquely by your genetic endowment and your personal choices. And your personal choices were shaped significantly by the choices of "significant others" in your life—especially your parents.

Understanding your childhood family environment and how it influences you today will mean seeing it through adult eyes. You might remember many of the basic facts about your childhood, but you might see them only through the eyes of a frightened child. In effect, you are living your life based on choices you made as a confused, and perhaps abused, child with a distorted view of reality. You need wisdom and insight to gain a truthful perspective on your past and present and to have an accurate context for changing your future.

Looking Back and Moving Forward

Perhaps you are feeling stuck and want to move forward in your life journey by making some new, healthier choices. As you begin to make changes, it is essential to recognize the obstacles and barriers constructed in your childhood family that might interfere with that process. In effect, you need to survey the damage and losses in your life before you begin to rebuild. That's what Nehemiah did. If you read Nehemiah 2:11-18, you'll see that he surveyed the destruction before rebuilding the Jerusalem wall.

Let's be clear about one thing at the outset. I am not saying you should live a past-focused life forever. On the contrary, you need to look at the past to untangle the knot of confusion and lies *so that you can move forward.*

As you begin this brief look back at your dysfunctional "family of origin," I invite you to consider Psalm 51:6. The God of Truth calls you to have truth in your inner person. He knows that some of that truth is stashed in dark corners of your mind that are hidden from your awareness. And God promises to give you wisdom in the hidden part he knows you need to see.

Time Out

It has been said that an unexamined life is not worth living. It might also be hazardous to your health and to the health of those closest to you! Especially as you loyally and thoughtlessly repeat painful patterns learned in childhood.

Right this moment, pause in your reading and pray your own versions of the following prayers:

☐ Lord, make me willing to see into the "hidden part" of my childhood.

☐ Lord, give me insight and wisdom about my past and how it influences my present.

Perhaps you didn't get past the first prayer. Obviously it would be foolish to fake this with yourself or with God, and I know this can be very scary. But would you ask God to make you *willing to be willing* to see the truth about your family that might be hidden from your conscious thoughts? It might help if you remember that we are not out to blame our parents for all our problems. We are after truth.

As a child in a dysfunctional family, you had no way of recognizing the chaos and craziness going on around you. After all, you were born into only *one* family—not an unhealthy family as well as a healthy one so you could compare the two. Therefore, you might not recognize the differences between functional and dysfunctional families.

Comparing Functional and Dysfunctional Families

Functional families are *not* problem-free families. What distinguishes functional from *dys*functional families is how they handle the inevitable problems they encounter.

Parents in functional families know that problems are a normal part of living in a sinful world. They work toward solving the problems and acknowledging the painful emotions that might accompany them. Parents in dysfunctional families deny problems and emotional pain. To preserve the illusion that the family is perfect, these parents expend their energy on *appearance management* instead of problem solving.

In functional families, parents are emotionally available to their children because they have learned to deal with their own emotions. Thus, they are able to help their children learn to handle their feelings instead of shaming the children for experiencing emotions.

When children experience trauma in well-functioning families, parents acknowledge the reality of the trauma. And while children in functional families encounter traumatic experiences occasionally, there is sufficient time between these experiences to resolve one before another hits.

In healthy families, parents adapt to their children's developmental needs, and they help the children mature appropriately. In dysfunctional families, children are forced to adapt to their parents' situational needs.

Describing Dysfunction

Families perform three basic functions to meet their members' needs:

1. *Maintenance*—meeting physical needs of food, shelter, clothing and medical care.

2. *Nurturance*—meeting emotional and relational needs for acceptance, affection, affirmation and time with others.

3. *Guidance*—meeting intellectual and spiritual needs for instruction on such enormously diverse topics as how to tie a shoe and how to know God.

A family is dysfunctional when it is marked by consistently inadequate or impaired functioning in meeting these needs. What makes a family's functioning inadequate or impaired? Consider who in the family has the primary responsibility for maintenance, nurturance and guidance. Surely, it can't be the children! Scripture and logic clearly teach that parents have the primary responsibility. Therefore, parents' inadequate and impaired functioning determine the degree that the family is impaired. Obviously, the degree varies from family to family just as it varies from person to person.

Impaired Parents

There are no perfect families. There are no perfect parents. But most parents, although imperfect, are *consistently adequate* in fulfilling their parenting responsibilities to provide safety, security and stability for their children. However, addictive and compulsive behaviors turn even the most loving parents into people who are unpredictable, unreliable and emotionally unavailable to their children.

Consistently adequate parents are committed to teaching their children about reality as truthfully as possible. Impaired parents consistently distort and deny large chunks of reality to conceal addictions and compulsions such as abusive and/or incestuous actions, chemical dependencies and/or workaholism. Much of the distortion and denial of reality concerns the unrealistic expectations parents project on their children.

Whether the denial is done ignorantly or purposefully, the effect is the same: children from dysfunctional families are handicapped personally, relationally and spiritually. Living with this handicap is like wearing a huge ball and chain labeled *shame*.

Teaching Shame

How do impaired parents shackle their offspring with shame? Obviously, when parents are so profoundly impaired that they sexually and/or physically abuse their children, these parents are teaching shame. But less severely impaired parents might also teach shame with their consistently unrealistic expectations.

The progression from parents' unrealistic expectations to an adult child's shame-based living goes something like this:

1. As a child, you were small and weak and hadn't yet learned to do

all the things your parents could do, so they seemed like gods. They were big and strong. They knew how to tie their shoes and to subtract. You concluded that your parents knew the truth about *everything*.

2. Therefore, you believed that their unrealistic expectations of you actually were based on the reality that "good" children are *perfect* children without developmental limitations and legitimate childhood needs. These *perfect* children would be able to *perfectly* please your parents because these children never track mud into the house, wet the bed, get less than an A, come in second at anything, arrive late, get a speeding ticket (or a divorce), or have children who do any of the above. It seemed reasonable. After all, your parents seemed perfect. And why would they expect you to be perfect if you weren't *supposed* to be perfect?

3. Since the chances are pretty good that you did some of those unacceptable things, you were forced to face your lack of perfection. You learned to feel different from and less than other people that you assumed were perfect.

An Example of Teaching Shame

I was standing in line in a crowded public rest room engaged in one of my favorite hobbies, people-watching, when I observed a brief interaction between a mother and daughter. Mother looked harried and weary as she wrestled a huge purse in one hand and a cigarette in the other while waiting for her child to emerge from a toilet stall. When the girl did, the beautiful, bright-eyed daughter marched over to a row of sinks to wash her hands dutifully. On the way, she dropped the jacket she was carrying. Mother snatched it from the floor and shot off a disgusted look which missed its mark since her daughter was engrossed in enthusiastic hand-washing. Water and soapsuds splashed on the mirror, sink, floor, and child while she scrubbed as if about to perform open-heart surgery. Again, mother released a nonverbal volley of disgust. Finally, the little beauty finished drying her hands and turned around with self-satisfaction and delight bursting from her face, only to be assaulted by her mother's inescapable barrage of displeasure, disgust and disappointment. Mother scolded, punched her child's shoulder and pointed to the water and suds (and then threw in care lessness with her jacket for good measure). She hit her target dead center this time. While the girl was being shoved out the door, her eyes seemed to bleed with sorrow and shame as she cast an apprehensive glance at her angry mother.

The mother's attitudes, actions and words conveyed to her daughter that the child was a disgusting disappointment when she accidentally dropped a jacket and splashed water and soapsuds. In reality, both behaviors are quite unremarkable for a child her age. Mother's behavior betrayed her unrealistic expectations; they needlessly fostered a sense of shame in her child.

By the way, this mother did not show her daughter how to wipe off the mirror and sink after her hand-washing. Instead of teaching the useful skill of cleaning up after oneself, Mother taught another lesson in shame. No doubt, this was a lesson Mother had been taught as a child herself.

From Generation to Generation

This family vignette illustrates the intergenerational aspect of shame. The mother's furtive glances at those of us in line betrayed her shame at having such an obviously imperfect child. It is likely that, from a young age, Mother's parents taught her the "you should be perfect" lie about herself and her future offspring. And, like a well-trained relay runner, Mother was passing on the family's intergenerational baton of shame. "Shame-passing" seems to be one of the malevolent "skills" taught in dysfunctional families.

Do you carry an intergenerational baton of shame? If your parents shamed you, it is probably because *they* were shamed by *their* parents. And so the wretched relay continues . . . "unto the third and fourth generations" and beyond.

Personal Reflection
□ As you read the comparison of functional and dysfunctional fam-

ilies on pages 38-39, which descriptions seemed more familiar?

☐ In what ways did you see your parents being shamed by their parents?

☐ In what ways did your parents pass the "baton of shame" to you?

☐ If you are a parent, in what ways are you passing shame to your children?

Looking Ahead

As we have seen, dysfunctional families teach shame. Perhaps you are beginning to identify the dysfunction in your family and the shame you were taught.

If you want to end the intergenerational shame-passing in your family, first you need to recognize that it is occurring. You also need to understand the family rules that preserve and promote shame-passing. We examine these rules in chapter four.

4
Rules in Dysfunctional Families

Rules in shame-based, dysfunctional families aren't the kind your mom writes out and posts on the refrigerator door with heart-shaped magnets. These are unwritten rules intended to conceal family imperfections because parents were taught that they and their children should be perfect. The rules help preserve the equilibrium of the family by protecting the parents from facing their personal problems. Trouble is, once you learn the rules, they're hard to forget, even if you leave your childhood family. Whether you are sixteen or sixty, if you are from a dysfunctional family, these rules are engraved in your mind.

After growing up in one dysfunctional family and observing scores of others, it seems to me they all have unrecorded rules that are variations of the following five:

Rule 1: Be blind.

Rule 2: Be quiet.

Rule 3: Be numb.
Rule 4: Be careful.
Rule 5: Be good.

Rule 1: Be Blind.

"Be blind" teaches children in unhealthy families to ignore the negative things that happen in the family. This rule also instructs them not to see or remember the ways their parents distort reality.

☐ *Be blind to your own perceptions of reality.* One child with an alcoholic father remembers asking her mother why her dad was sleeping on the front lawn. The mother replied, "Daddy's camping out." In reality, he had been so intoxicated the night before, he had passed out attempting to get up the porch steps.

Many times the distortions place the blame on the child. Do either of the following sound familiar?

"You're so clumsy—always falling down and hurting yourself." (The child's bruises were really the result of the mother's angry beating .)

"You're crazy if you think we're not a good Christian family!" (This came in response to the question, "Why aren't we happy at home when we're so happy at church?")

Because no one wants to be "crazy," children receiving such replies learn to ignore everything that does not match their parents' perceptual demands. Besides, children cannot risk alienating their adult caregivers by continually disputing the adults' distorted interpretations of reality. It literally is a matter of life and death to young children who would not survive abandonment by their parents. Even children old enough to care for themselves fear the painful *emotional* abandonment they experience when they fail to live by the family rules—including "be blind." So children learn to surrender their own perceptions.

Parental distortion of reality is actually a form of *intellectual* child abuse. As adults, these intellectually abused children might seek endless validation of every decision. They automatically assume *they* are wrong whenever someone expresses an opinion different from theirs. And these adult children, taught to mistrust their own perceptions, are ripe to fall for religious "gurus" and secular "experts" who profitably promote *their* perceptions as truth with a capital *T*. This might be one reason that adolescent and adult children from dysfunctional families are attracted to strong, charismatic cult leaders.

The "be blind" rule applies to more than just parental distortions and denial of fact. Children in dysfunctional families are expected to be blind to their parents' confusing mixed messages.

☐ *Be blind to mixed messages.* Communication in dysfunctional families has been called "crazy-making" because it is characterized by mixed messages that contradict logic and confuse listeners—especially children. Art was one of those children.

Art remembers, "I never knew who I was or where I stood with my folks. I often heard my dad tell his drinking buddies, 'I'm proud of that rotten, no-good kid.' "

Art always wondered which part of the message was true. Was he worthwhile or was he rotten and no good? All he really knew was that he was confused and that he was supposed to be blind to the source of his confusion. At thirty-seven, Art is just beginning to recognize his alcoholic father's mixed messages as the origin of his identity confusion.

Art also is no longer blind to the adult role he was forced to play as a child. As his dad's alcoholism progressed, Art took over more and more responsibilities as the "man of the house." But, of course, Art was not supposed to see that he was parenting his parents.

☐ *Be blind to role reversals.* Dysfunctional families are populated by "adultified" children and "childified" adults. In these homes, parents often use their children to meet distorted needs for power, nurturing and even sexual gratification, while the children's needs are ignored. To maintain their place in the family and avoid physical and/or emotional abandonment, children learn early to meet their parents' needs for parenting. Barbara was such a child.

Looking back, Barbara doesn't remember ever feeling like a child. "I think I was born going on thirty-five. My mother was always overwhelmed and depressed because of my dad's drinking. I would try to clean up his messes and help her out as much as I could. She told me over and over how disgusted she was by him and his sexual advances and, in the next breath, how we wouldn't make it if he left us. When he started crawling into bed with me—all groping hands and foul smells, I knew I had to let him do that stuff between my legs so he'd let my mom alone but keep coming home."

It is pretty terrifying to see that you are taking care of your parents emotionally and sexually. So Barbara learned to "be blind." And as all incest survivors, and most adult children know, you are expected to be quiet about what you did not see.

Rule 2: Be Quiet.

Dysfunctional families are loaded with secrets. There is a world of difference between a surprise and a secret. Surprises are healthy and fun because they include *temporarily* withholding information for a clearly determined time. Dad and little Susie shopping for Mommy's Christmas present and not telling her about it is an example of a surprise. Susie is not frightened or confused because she knows Mommy will be happy when she finds out all about it on December 25.

In contrast, secrets have enormous destructive potential. Destructive secrets always involve at least three people. Dad asking little Mary to rub his penis and then securing her promise never to tell Mommy about it is an example of a destructive secret. Mary is very frightened and confused because she would like to ask her mother to tell Daddy to stop. But Mary doesn't want Mommy to be unhappy, and that's what Daddy said would happen if Mary ever told.

Remember, all the dysfunctional family rules serve to preserve the equilibrium of the family by protecting impaired parents from facing their personal problems. By obeying the "be quiet" rule and keeping the secret of sexual abuse, Mary protects Dad from the consequences of his incestuous behavior, and she protects Mom from being upset.

I recently read about a dramatic example of the "be quiet" rule's function to protect impaired parents. In a study of fourteen adolescent males on death row, the researchers observed that:

Eight of the 14 had injuries severe enough to require hospitalization. . . . Twelve had been brutally abused and five had been sodomized by relatives. Their parents had a high rate of alcoholism, drug abuse, and psychiatric hospitalization. The boys had tried to conceal all this during their trials. They preferred to be seen as bad rather than admit that they were . . . victims of . . . abuse. *The parents often cooperated with the prosecution (and even urged the death sentence) because they had an interest in concealing their own actions.*[1]
Apparently, these parents were more invested in preserving their images than in preserving their sons' lives.]

The "be quiet" rule applies inside and outside the family, and it extends to nonverbal as well as verbal communication.

□ *Be quiet in public.* A favorite motto in dysfunctional families is: "Children should be seen and not heard"; children are tutored in the "be quiet" rule in the name of "family loyalty."

When interacting with the outside world, impaired parents model the family's top priority: looking perfect. This is accomplished by keeping up appearances, based on the belief that what matters most is not how you (and the family) *are,* but how you (and the family) *look.* And the more unhealthy the family, the more energy is invested in keeping up appearances (appearance management). Little or no energy is spent on problem-solving.

In a family like that, children soon learn how rigid the "be quiet" rule is outside the family. Beth certainly did.

Beth's father was a prominent pastor in a small western community. Beth's father was also physically abusive. If Beth's family had been functioning in an adequate and appropriate manner, her father would have sought help to change when he recognized that he was beginning to express his rage by kicking and punching his children. Beth's mother would have protected her children and confronted her husband. Whether he obtained professional or lay counseling, Beth's father would have been willing to be accountable for practicing strategies designed to change his abusive behavior. Perhaps the entire family would have gone for counseling. At any rate, the emphasis would have been on solving the problem. That's not how Beth remembers the family's focus.

"I used to wonder why my mother was more concerned with my father's reputation and 'ruining the family's testimony in the community' than she was with how much pain I felt. Honestly, there were times when my arms and legs looked like a Picasso! When the bruises were really colorful, the solution was always the same—wear leotards and long-sleeved dresses. (My mother and father were too spiritual to allow girls to wear slacks.) Even during miserably hot summers, I had to wear long sleeves and thick leotards to hide my bruised arms and legs. I don't really remember being told to keep quiet about Dad's abusiveness. I just knew what was expected of me. Besides, I loved Jesus and sure didn't want to be the one to ruin our family's Christian witness."

The "be quiet in public" rule often accompanies children into their adult lives. After years of chronic depression, self-sabotaging behavior and spiritual barrenness, Beth finally talked with a lay-counselor in her church. However, when the counselor suggested that Beth would benefit from attending a group for Christian adults raised in dysfunctional families, Beth abruptly ended counseling.

For many people like Beth, the adult child version of "be quiet in public" is translated: "Never get any help for yourself." Personal and spiritual healing are sacrificed on the altar of "family loyalty."

☐ *Be quiet at home.* One of the most striking characteristics of dysfunctional families is that their members often do not discuss the family's pain even with each other. Children in unhealthy families soon learn that any comments about family problems or questions about family secrets are denied and deflected.

Self-protective parents use ingenious methods to enforce the "be quiet at home" rule. One of the most effective is enlarging and enshrining of the family's "good times."

When a child complains about [family] pain, the child might quickly be reminded of a holiday celebration some years ago when there were 40 people for dinner and a three-piece band. These parents are telling their children to forget and deny that pain exists. This family clings to one another in a desperate and dishonest way, attempting to prove closeness.[2]

The first rule directed children in dysfunctional families to be blind by relinquishing their own perceptions of reality. The second rule builds on that faulty foundation by demanding that these children be quiet about their disowned perceptions. The third rule adds the next logical injunction: "Don't feel what you don't see and don't discuss."

Rule 3: Be Numb.

Leprosy, or Hansen's disease, damages the body's ability to register physical pain to such an extent that leprous babies sometimes chew off their fingers because they feel no pain. If they reach adulthood, these children will be missing vital, God-designed portions of their physical selves.

☐ *Be numb to feelings.* Dysfunctional families both stimulate strong emotions and block their expression. Children in these families seem to develop a kind of "emotional leprosy" or numbness that allows them to block out their confusing, often overwhelming feelings.

Research on brain functioning suggests that people who are taught in childhood to repress (unconsciously block) their emotions have a lag in the time it takes for certain information about feelings to get from one side of their brains to the other. However, the lag was only for *disturbing* messages about emotions such as anxiety and anger. Apparently, the brain learned to hinder awareness of painful emotions.

We have seen already that young children learn to accommodate the needs of their impaired parents in order to avoid abandonment and stay attached to the family. Very early, these children realize that their parents cannot tolerate displays of anger, sadness, fear or pain. Expressions of those emotions betray the family secret that all is not perfect. Therefore, disturbing emotions become enemies to be feared and eventually numbed and repressed.

Adults who repress emotions often are unable to answer the question, "How do you feel about that?" with anything more specific than

"I don't know." In effect, they have sacrificed God-given parts of their emotional selves to survive their chaotic and/or traumatic childhoods.

Lingering awareness of disturbing emotions is shamed in most dysfunctional families. For example, children in these homes often grew up hearing, "You shouldn't feel like that," to their expressions of hurt and anger in response to genuinely inappropriate and even abusive treatment.

Even strong, *pleasant* emotions are shamed in some families. Many adults raised in dysfunctional families headed by Christian parents have told me that they were shamed for experiencing joy. Their parents would ask, "How can you be so frivolous [or selfish] when there is so much suffering in the world?"

In effect, shaming parents send a loud and clear message: "Your emotions don't count." Impaired parents also send a "yours don't count" message about their children's personal boundaries.

□ *Be numb to personal boundaries.* Our personal boundaries help us know where we end, where others begin and who we are in relation to them. When our personal boundaries are well defined, we know that we have separate feelings, perceptions and opinions, and we are comfortable with that. Without healthy boundaries, we will not know when we are being invaded and/or abused.

Clearly, physical and sexual abuse are devastating violations of a child's personal boundary. And children in dysfunctional, abusive families are expected to accept such boundary violations.

But children's personal boundaries are often violated in the name of love. One of my favorite examples is of the woman who told her child, "I'm cold. Put on your sweater." Obviously, this mother had learned to numb her own boundaries and was teaching her child to do the same.

I'm sure you already have discovered that these Dysfunctional Family Rules interact and overlap. For example, if your physical, sexual and/or intellectual boundaries were violated in childhood, you were expected to numb your boundary edges, numb your feelings about the violations, be blind to your perceptions about it and be quiet about the entire episode.

I'm sure too that if you were raised in a dysfunctional family, with or without overt abuse, you discovered your need to master Rule 4.

Rule 4: Be Careful.

A philosopher once asked, "Is the universe friendly?" At birth, we are enrolled in a school intended to teach us the answer. That school is called a family.

The dysfunctional family's universe is not very friendly for the children in it. You might have discovered that years ago. Sometimes it isn't even very safe. And even if it is safe for arms, legs and genitals, it might not be safe for ideas, opinions and aspirations. Therefore if you were raised by impaired parents, you learned to survive by obeying the "be careful" rule.

From what you've learned already about dysfunctional families, you can understand why the children in them learn to be careful. Impaired parents typically function in an inconsistent, unreliable manner. Depending on their degrees of personal impairment, parents create families that their children experienced as unpredictable, chaotic and/or unsafe.

This rule addresses issues of trust, and it is difficult for children to learn to trust when their parents are consistently inconsistent. If you are one of these children, you tend to distrust people's intentions toward you. And frequently, God is "tarred with the same brush" when it comes to distrusting.[3] If you are an adult child from a dysfunctional family, you might hear yourself say something like, "If I want it done right, I'll have to do it myself," or, "No, no, I don't need any help, I can handle it myself." (I know an adult child of an alcoholic who actually carried a huge desk down three flights of stairs by himself while refusing sincere offers of help!) You also might remember that, as a child, you learned to spot clues to determine the safety of your surroundings. Today you might be quite the expert at reading people and situations. Bonnie is one woman who illustrates this.

Bonnie's father never laid a hand on her. But he shredded her self-concept with his scathing verbal assaults whenever she displeased him.

"I knew whether or not it was going to be a good evening by the way my dad arched his eyebrows when he came home after work. My eyes were riveted on his face to see if he would be looking for things to criticize in me and the other kids. I learned to 'take cover' when his face said 'look out; here it comes.' It is kind of funny that my friends think of me as such a discerning and sensitive person. I am beginning to see myself as still 'on guard' against being hurt."

In effect, Bonnie sees herself as a good (and tired) scout who must stay prepared because the other shoe is always about to drop. No wonder Bonnie has to be careful. As a child, Bonnie knew nothing about these Dysfunctional Family Rules, yet she recalls trying fervently to master Rule Five.

Rule 5: Be Good.

In dysfunctional families the word *good,* when applied to children, is actually a code word for *perfect.*

The truth is that if parents are distracted by their own personal pain, the last thing they need or want is a real, human child with all his or her developmental limitations and legitimate needs. Instead of age-appropriate children, impaired parents actually want and need permanent-press "short adults" who can pass for children!

What did it take to be called "good" if you were raised in a dysfunctional family? Here are some of the mandatory requirements. (If impaired parents could advertise for their children, this list would comprise the child's job description.)

A "good" child:
1. never inconveniences parents
2. never embarrasses or disappoints parents
3. never has personal needs
4. knows how to do everything correctly without being taught
5. never has a critical or separate thought
6. never loses (except when competing with a parent)
7. never gets less than an A in any class in any grade for any reason
8. thrives on instability, chaos and pain

9. does everything parents ask (joyfully, instantly and perfectly, of course)

10. never remembers anything but the "happy times"

Unrealistic expectations, you say? Of course they are, but that doesn't stop children from believing that they *should* be able to meet them.

The Shame of Not "Being Good"

He was short, dark and handsome. Around and around he quietly trotted, following the intricate Indian designs in the carpet of the Phoenix airport. He didn't yell or cry. He didn't disturb or wander away from his young mother, but she expected much more of her three-year-old son. "Stop that, you little bastard. I told you to come and sit down right here. I mean it, damn you. Why do you have to be so bad?"

Chin on chest, the small boy walked slowly toward his mother. She snatched him off the floor and pushed him down into the chair beside her. "Now, sit there and *be good!*" He began to swing his legs, but his mother hit them with the book she had been reading. "Be good, I said. Damn you, be good."

I last saw the boy as his mother dragged him by one arm—feet skimming the floor—to their departure gate.

Can you see that the boy's behavior was appropriate for a three-year-old? Yet he was not allowed to be a carefree, curious, creative child. He was forced to adapt to his mother's need for him to be a "short adult." He failed to do that perfectly and was called "bad," among other things.

To have been considered a "good child" by his mother, this boy would have had to be no child at all.

The Rules in Poetry and Pain

The following poem was written by an anonymous incest survivor. As you read the poem on the left, see how many of the Dysfunctional Family Rules you can identify without looking at the list on the right.

"Hush, Little Baby"	Family Rules
Hush, little baby, don't you cry:	Be numb/Be quiet
Close your eyes, don't breathe a sigh.	Be blind/Be quiet
Don't pay no heed to what we try;	Be blind/Be numb
Ain't no one at all on whom to rely.	Be careful
Good little baby, you didn't cry;	Be good
You did what we said, even stifled your sigh.	Be good/Be numb/ Be quiet
Beg again, you can go, by-and-by,	
We'll just say that you're telling a lie.	Be blind/Be quiet
Poor little baby, guess your mind went awry;	
You still cain't [sic] never, ever even cry.	Be quiet/Be numb
Sure don't know why you didn't die;	
Instead, spent a lifetime asking, "Why?"	Be blind (doesn't trust own perceptions)

Time Out

Remember to pray for "wisdom in the hidden parts" as you consider the following questions. The more dysfunctional the family in which you were raised, the more difficult it will be for you to remember the *whole* picture, because you might have been taught that "good" children only remember the "happy times." And you've always wanted to be "good."

Personal Reflection

☐ What are some of the rules you learned in your family as a child?

☐ How did these rules contribute to unrealistic expectations and a sense of shame?

☐ Complete the following sentences. The first one identifies what was demanded of you in your family, and the second identifies what was forbidden.

1. I was a "good" child when I did/was _____

2. I was a "good" child when I did not/was not _____

Looking Ahead

This chapter has focused on the similarities in dysfunctional families by examining the unspoken rules that govern them. However, each dysfunctional family system is unique, and each falls somewhere along a continuum from mildly to extremely dysfunctional.

In chapter five we will look at levels of family dysfunction and shaming and at levels of abuse.

5
Abuse and Shaming in Dysfunctional Families

*T*he Lord is my shepherd; I shall not want," begins the much-loved Twenty-third Psalm (KJV). The loving care of shepherds is so legendary that we immediately respond to the image of the Good Shepherd. But imagine instead a cruel shepherd who tortures his lambs and then flings them over a cliff. This would be the same unnatural situation that occurs when overtly abusive parents thrust their children into adulthood with gaping wounds that leave the children vulnerable to further abuses.

In less dramatic ways, other parents abdicate their shepherding roles by spiritually, intellectually, and/or emotionally abandoning their "lambs." This rupture in the protective parental fence leaves children exposed to foolish and dangerous wanderings.

I have counseled adults who have experienced levels of parental shaming that range from Satanic ritualistic abuse to unintentional emotional neglect. But I hesitate to place any two persons' abuses side by side. There is an inherent danger in any attempt to describe "levels" of abuse. This approach risks minimizing and discounting the pain of children in less overtly dysfunctional families. Nevertheless, for the sake of organizing the following material, I will label overt abuse as observable invasion of a child's body. Overt abuse takes the form of physical abuse and/or most forms of sexual abuse.

A child receives all parental actions and attitudes as messages about the child's identity. The more overt the abuse, the clearer the shamefull message conveys: "You are a worthless child who deserves this treatment because you are intrinsically different and less valuable than other children." That message is the very essence of shame.

Physical Abuse

Impaired parents are amazingly creative in their varied expressions of physical abuse. Some of its many forms include shaking or squeezing the child; throwing or slamming the child against walls or objects; beating the child with one's hands or object; burning or scalding the child; confining the child in boxes or closets; or forcing or withholding food and/or water. The supposed offenses deserving the abuse can be amazingly small. Carla's story is typical.

"It happened so many times I couldn't keep track. But for some reason, one time sticks out in my mind. We were sitting at the dinner table, and I spilled my milk. My dad leaped out of his chair, grabbed me, threw me on the floor and began kicking me. I remember his face was red, his teeth were clenched, and I thought he was going to kill me." Carla paused, then added softly, "I mean, all I did was spill my milk, for heaven's sakes. Is that such a crime?"

Carla described her mother coming into her room later to explain that her father was "under a lot of pressure at work."

"She told me that I needed to try harder to make supper a more pleasant family time. And you know the crazy part? I believed she was right. I was forty years old before I started learning that it wasn't my fault."

Physical abuse doesn't need to include physical contact. When an intoxicated father takes his children for a high-speed ride on a mountain road at night with the headlights off, that is abuse. And if you are a witness to the physical abuse of someone else, you are a victim of abuse as well—*vicarious abuse*.

Sexual Abuse

Sexual abuse of children has been called the crime of the 1990s. Dr. Robert Geffner of the University of Texas' Family Violence Research and Treatment Program believes that one of every four girls will be sexually abused *within the family* by age eighteen. With boys, the chances are one in eight, Dr. Geffner stated.

[Geffner] calls the prevalence of sexual abuse incidents across the USA "staggering." "There's nothing more traumatic to a child," he says. *"All our cultural values of love, sex, family values and role boundaries are all mixed up and turned upside-down."*[1]

Turned upside-down, indeed, for in an incestuous family, a child becomes "good" by becoming "bad." The childhood of one woman I know poignantly illustrates this. Charlotte remembers feeling bad—very, very bad.

"I hated sitting in Sunday-school class and church pretending I was just like the other kids, but my folks never missed a Sunday. My dad was a deacon. The worst times were when our minister would preach on adultery. I was ten years old, and I knew that I was guilty of adultery because my father was having intercourse with me several times a week. I felt so disgustingly filthy. I was always amazed that people couldn't see it in my face. I tried to make him stop, but he told me that he loved me and said I was a good girl for letting him show me in 'our special way.' "

The "be good" rule in Charlotte's family included unquestioning obedience to a sexually abusive father which left her confused about herself, her family and her God.

Sexual abuse of children goes beyond intercourse to fondling, sexual touching, exposing oneself or masturbating in front of a child, mutual masturbation, oral sex and anal sex. In addition, penetration with fingers or objects, forcing children to have sex with each other, forcing sexual activity with animals, taking pornographic pictures of children and forcing children to watch pornography or others being sexually abused are examples of sexual abuse. Even where these activities do not occur, an incestuous, sexually-charged atmosphere characterizes a home were there are sexual jokes, innuendoes, leering and "games."

Dot's father refused to stop bathing her, even when she had begun to develop sexually. She remembers him scrubbing her genitals until they burned. When she begged to be allowed to take showers like other girls her age, her father insisted on staying in the bathroom to watch her "so she would not fall and hurt herself." This father never allowed the family to use a shower curtain or lock the bathroom door. Dot always felt "weird" about her dad's "wet and sloppy kisses and long, tight hugs" but she never connected her perceptions to the many personal boundary violations she experienced in her incestuous family.

Emotional Incest

For Sue Ann, the incest was the non-contact, subtle form commonly called emotional incest. Sue Ann recalls getting attention from her father only when she was being "cutesy and flirty." As an adult, Sue Ann tends to sexualize her relationships with men in positions of authority.

Emotional incest can also occur when parents are emotionally or legally divorced and a parent treats an opposite-sex child like a "little spouse." Brent's mother used him for a confidante and companion after his father left home.

"Mom often crawled into bed with me to talk about how lonely she was. You can't imagine how confused and scared I felt when I had an erection one time when she was snuggled up next to me."

While emotional incest represents a "subtle" form of the sexual abuse, other forms include unimaginable brutality.

Sexual and Physical Abuse Combined

Frequently, sexual abuse is accompanied by physical abuse, either by the same or the other parent. Wanda's father was brutally abusive in his sexual assaults on her. As a Christian adult in a loving marriage, she now feels safe enough to remember the burning, the beatings and other sexual horrors she endured at her father's hands.

For Yvonne, the situation was a little different. "I am ashamed to admit it, but having intercourse with my father was no big deal. In fact, it was kind of calm and peaceful compared to the things my mother did to me."

Yvonne's childhood resembled life in a concentration camp. Rarely a night passed that her schizophrenic mother did not awaken her to inflict some creative, new form of torture. Sometimes it was inserting a broom handle into Yvonne's anus and making her keep it there all night. Other times Yvonne was starved and then forced to eat human excrement. Is it any wonder that, to Yvonne, her father's incestuous acts seemed inconsequential in comparison to her mother's physical abuse?

It might seem that we've plumbed the depths of overt abuse and shaming when we consider the plight of children abused both sexually and physically as were Wanda and Yvonne. Yet there is another hideous form of child abuse that includes those abuses while adding elements of unspeakable horror.

Satanic Ritualistic Abuse

"Do you think it would be bad to kill babies and see them skinned? I thought it was pretty bad at first. But then I told myself, 'Oh, that's not so bad. I can take it.'" And Zoe did take it for years as she was ritualistically raped, sodomized and forced to participate in the murder and cannibalization of infants. Zoe's parents worshiped Satan.

Satanic ritualistic abuse is an unbelievably brutal form of child treatment involving sexual, physical, psychological and spiritual abuse. Children are subjected to terrifying rituals, mind-altering drugs and techniques, and/or grisly threats to confuse and control them. Often, adults force the victim to participate in ritualistic murder and mutilation to create a sense of personal guilt and guarantee the victim's silence.

In the past few years the media has reported cases of ritualistic abuse occurring in preschools and day-care facilities. As traumatic as that experience would be for a young child, imagine the unspeakable horror of being trapped in a home where your own parents are the ritualistic abusers. That was Zoe's experience.

As a child Zoe maintained her sanity by dividing her experiences of ritualistic abuse into many separate segments of her mind. For twenty years this enabled her to totally block the memories. But that didn't erase the messages the abuse delivered: You are different from other children, and God will never love you. Zoe also learned that the world is not a safe place because adults can be murderously cruel.

Miraculously, God's grace rescued Zoe. Now as a Christian adult, Zoe travels a torturous road strewn with enormous obstacles to knowing her heavenly Father's love.

Even if not forced into Satanic worship as children, adolescents or adults, those of us from dysfunctional families are susceptible to occultic promises of power and control. *Changes,* a magazine "for and about adult children," recently reported that Satanists are attempting to proselytize recovering adults. One expert in this area believes that "12-step groups need to protect their vulnerable members from Satanic exploitation."[2]

Time Out

I urge you to stop right this moment and renounce any current or previous involvement in occultic or Satanic activities. Appendix A (p. 191) lists occultic practices that might open a person to Satanic influences. It also includes a prayer of renunciation. You might want to seek the help of your pastor or a spiritually mature friend to pray with you.

"So far so good," you might be saying to yourself. "These descriptions of overt abuses have been informative but not particularly relevant to me."

As we turn a corner to look at the more subtle, non-contact forms of abuse and shaming in dysfunctional families, you might become uncomfortably aware that some of this sounds familiar. Remember, this look at your family is designed to provide a context for changing painful "stuck" places in your life. And these non-contact abuses might not disfigure visibly, but they leave unseen scars that mark your life and family even if everything looks good.

"Look So Good" Families

"Look so good" families do just that—they look *so* good. However, on closer inspection you find that they don't function so well. Their family motto is: *what will the neighbors think?* And, of course, this family presents itself in such a way that the neighbors typically think it looks very good indeed. Nevertheless, these families are shame-based and shame-bound. Parents in "look so good" families usually are less severely impaired than those in overtly abusing families. For example, Father might be workaholic instead of alcoholic, and Mother might be chronically sad rather than clinically depressed.

If you are from a "look so good" family, you probably grew up being controlled by emotional and verbal abuse. As a result, you might have many of the same symptoms experienced by adults raised in overtly abusive homes. I've had many adult children from "look so good" families tell me they feel "crazy" because they cannot remember any "real" bodily-contact abuse. Yet they closely identify with "adult child" issues.

Just as physical and sexual abuse are expressed in a variety of ways, emotional and verbal abuse take many forms. Some of these include ridiculing, belittling, name-calling, negatively comparing, publicly humiliating, overprotecting, excessively blaming, and/or transferring blame onto a child. Here are some of the subtle and creative shaming strategies I've observed in dysfunctional but "look so good" families.

Emotional Orphaning

Terry is an abuse survivor, but you have to look in his sad eyes to see the scars.

"I hear people complain that they don't remember their dads ever saying 'I love you' to them. Man, that's nothing. I don't remember my dad ever saying *anything* to me. I used to think I had this magical power to become invisible, but it only seemed to work at home. My mom was close with my sisters, but she never seemed to want to connect to me, so she usually kept her distance. And my dad always looked right through me. I used to wonder what was wrong with me that I couldn't seem to get my folks to notice me. At first I tried to get noticed by doing everything I thought a good kid would do. When that didn't work, I sort of gave up and drifted into the drug scene. They didn't seem to care either way."

Terry's dysfunctional family proved that parents don't have to be dead to orphan children. Some impaired parents "orphan" their children by deliberately using emotional withdrawal and silence as punishment. This was probably how the parents were punished, so it is their method of choice. In other instances, parents are emotionally unavailable to their children unintentionally. Whatever their reason, these parents create emotional orphans.

You might have been emotionally orphaned by the absence of a father and a mother who were consistently overwhelmed. That's the picture seen in many families of divorce. And even when a mother is consistently competent and appropriately available to her children, she cannot replace an absent father.

Father Hunger

Because of divorce in this country, nearly a million more children each year live in homes without a father.[3] This father loss, or "father hunger," has a profound impact on children.

Girls need fathers to learn how to *relate* to men, and boys need fathers to learn how to *be* men. If you are a woman with father hunger, you might be starved for attention and affection from men—especially older men in positions of authority. Perhaps you've found yourself repeatedly exchanging sexual intercourse for the male embraces you crave. You don't intend to get into one sexual situation after another, it just seems to "happen."

If you are an adult son from a home without a father, you might have lacked a male role model to teach you how to handle aggressive impulses and how to develop social behavior appropriate to a man. You too probably crave attention and approval from male authority figures, and you might be willing to twist yourself into an emotional pretzel to get it.

Whether you are male or female, father loss profoundly affects your ability to trust the *heavenly* Father. And your spiritual struggles might be a source of deep shame if you don't understand the impact of father loss.

Hooking the Shame

Have you ever looked closely at a piece of Velcro? If you do, you will notice that one side of the Velcro is covered with tiny loops and the other side is composed of little hooks. When you bring the two sides together, the hooks grab the loops and hold on tight. The process I call "hooking the shame" works the same way.

In both overtly abusive and subtly abusive dysfunctional families, parents habitually and deliberately use shaming to control their children. In effect, these impaired parents implant "shame loops" in their children with verbal and nonverbal shaming messages. "Hooking the shame" occurs when parents use verbal and/or emotional pressure to attach their demands to the shame loops they created in their children. These parental "shame hooks" are perfectly fitted to the pre-existing shame loops, and the resulting bond gives a new and sinister definition to "the tie that binds."

Here are several examples of "hooking the shame."

☐ *Negative comparisons.* Obviously, any time a parent negatively compares a child to someone else, that hooks the child's sense of being different and less than others.

☐ *Declarations of shame.* Parents who were raised on a steady diet of "I'm so ashamed of you" regularly serve their children the same fare. The parent invariably adds, "You ought to be ashamed of yourself."

Those two tidbits of verbal abuse virtually guarantee intergenerational shame-passing because if you're a loyal child, the only decent thing you can do is be ashamed of yourself. That's why declarations of shame work so well.

□ *Redefining respect.* When children in dysfunctional families hear, "Respect your elders," they need to know that those are code-words meaning, "Have no thoughts, opinions or preferences that differ from those of your parents." *Respect your elders* might also be translated, "Do everything older relatives tell you to do and ask no questions."

This form of subtle abuse and shaming is extremely effective for controlling older children in dysfunctional families. This strategy requires that any attempts by children to separate appropriately from their parents and develop their own individuality must be redefined as "disrespecting your elders." Even *adult* children feel the powerful pull of this control strategy.

The group I lead for adult children from dysfunctional families was gearing up to face the holidays. We had been talking, laughing and crying about the challenges of visiting impaired parents without "growing down" too much. ("Growing down" is the phenomenon wherein you are age twenty-five, thirty-five or fifty when you return to your parents' home, but you emerge two or three days later *feeling* age six, eight or twelve.)

We laughed about how even minor issues become emotion-laden loyalty tests in dysfunctional families. If you were raised in one, you know what we mean. Here were some loyalty tests the group came up with. Have you ever been asked the equivalent of these accusations?

"Why in the world would you change Great-grandma's recipe for stuffing? You know *we always* use a cornbread base!"

"How could you think of visiting old high-school friends when you know *we always* watch football games all day on Thanksgiving?"

In both statements, *we always* is the verbal hook used to grab your sense of family loyalty. Dysfunctional parents redefine respect for elders to include everything from joining the same church to buying the same make of car "we always" do. In effect, mindless obedience to every spoken or unspoken parental pattern and preference becomes the litmus test for family loyalty. And there is a high emotional price to pay for failing.

While several group members agreed there was a "walking on egg shells" atmosphere around their parents, Virginia painted the scene in darker tones.

"In our house it was more like trying to tap dance through a mine field. My father terrorized the family with his anger. It was as if there was only one right way to do anything, and it was *his* way, of course. He seemed to take it as a personal insult if we did things differently. Anyone who has an opinion different from his is made to feel like a fool—or a traitor. You wouldn't believe the hell my husband and I went through when my father found out we bought a Honda. [Actually, the group had no trouble at all believing it!] We got the 'buy American' speech, ending with 'I guess my Chevy isn't good enough for big shots like you.' "

Group members nodded with understanding as Virginia paused to catch her breath. "I dread our Christmas trip to my folks' place but don't have the guts to stay home. I know I'll spend the entire day holding my breath around Dad, hoping no one says anything to set him off and ruin our Christmas."

In Virginia's family, *respect* was redefined to include both "spend holidays with your parents forever whether you want to or not," and "don't express any opinion or preference that differs from your father's or he'll explode and it will all be your fault that the day is ruined." Sound familiar? Perhaps you're still performing the intergenerational steps that choreograph your "tap dance" through the family's mine field. And since it is simply expected of you if you "respect your elders," you probably don't even get any praise for a good performance.

Praise for *anything* is often a scarce commodity in dysfunctional families, but that's not always the case. In these families praise might abound, but it might also subtly abuse.

□ *Praising without affirmation.* Walt was confused as he reflected on his childhood in an upper-middle-class family. An outstanding athlete and top student, Walt relished the attention and praise his parents lavished on him for every new accomplishment and award. Yet his parents never affirmed him as a person of intrinsic worth. As an adult, Walt is a driven, insecure, critical workaholic.

"It just doesn't make any sense to me. My folks were wonderful compared to some of the parents I hear about. So why do I feel so connected to all the stuff I'm hearing about self-hatred and codependent relationships? I'm really confused."

If you, like Walt, were nurtured on praise without affirmation, your life might have looked full, but inside you were empty. Maybe you still are.

Praise without affirmation focuses on performance, not personhood. If you were subtly abused by this technique, you might feel hollow because all of your parents' emphasis was on outward performance to the neglect of inner development. You might be a person who experiences yourself not as a human *being*, but as a human *doing*. In praise-without-affirmation families you hear phrases like: "Mommy loves Susie when she cleans up all her toys like that." Or, "I was never so proud of you, Dan, as the day you made the all-state team." You might also hear variations on the family motto: "second place is no place."

However, in these families, affirmation of intrinsic personal worth is scarce. Walt does not remember hearing, "I love you just because you are you." Do you remember such a statement? For no particular performance-related reason, did you ever hear something like, "I am so glad God gave you to us because you're such a swell kid"? Are you struggling to even *imagine* what it would be like to hear this from your folks? That's a clue that you probably never did.

Individuals who practice the praise-without-affirmation strategy graduated from the Vince Lombardi School of Parenting where they learned that "winning is the *only* thing." I met one of the honor graduates in the autumn of 1984.

My son, Dave, was the silver medalist in the 100 meter backstroke at the 1984 Summer Olympics in Los Angeles. As you can imagine, it was an exciting time for our entire family. The Olympic afterglow faded quickly as Dave put the medal away and moved on appropriately with his life. Still, old friends and new acquaintances "oohed" and "aahed" over Dave's achievement. One man's response stands out in my memory because he was the only person who ever called Dave a "loser." Well, of course, he didn't call him a "loser" directly. Here's what he said: "Yeah, we saw Dave's race on TV. It was sure close, in fact it looked like he was ahead coming out of the turn. We were sure hoping he'd win. Too bad he lost."

I remember so clearly the amazement and amusement I felt at that moment. It struck me as funny that *I had never thought of Dave as losing*. It isn't that I thought he finished first. It was just that I had never considered winning a silver Olympic medal as losing!

But if "second place is no place," then anything less than first place makes you a loser. Is that how you see life?

In praise-without-affirmation homes, the quality and closeness of children's relationships with their parents depends on their achievements rather than on their intrinsic worth. Elliott described how it worked when he was a child.

"I had an A or B relationship with my folks depending on my grades. Even later on it was the same way. When I dropped out of my master's program to get some practical experience, my folks demoted me to the B relationship and made it clear that I had deeply disappointed them. Of course, now that I've finished my Ph.D. and passed the licensing exam, I've been upgraded to A status."

As a child, Elliott received this shaming message loud and clear: "You have no intrinsic worth as a person created by God." He spent years jumping through academic hoops his parents held up before him. Now, Elliott is an extremely competent, caring psychologist specializing in family therapy. And he is working hard with his own children to change the parenting style he saw modeled as a child.

Personal Reflection

☐ As you consider your childhood, do you remember any non-contact emotional and/or verbal abuse?

☐ I realize this might be painful, but ask yourself if you remember any bodily-invasive, severe abuse in your childhood. *Remember, nothing that anyone ever did to you is a statement about your intrinsic worth. And nothing that anyone ever did to you disqualifies you from receiving all that God has for you.* With those two reminders in view, list any types of severe abuse you experienced as a child.

☐ If you are experiencing a great deal of anxiety and/or depression as you look into your past and examine your relationship with your parents, you might need to seek some support and encouragement. Of course, God is your ultimate source of strength, but he often uses human agents to minister that strength.

☐ Remember, you do not have to go through your pain alone *this* time. What resources do you have to provide support and encouragement (e.g., your pastor, a spiritually mature and sensitive [same-sex] friend, a Christian lay-counselor, a Christian mental health professional, a Christ-centered support group)?

Looking Ahead
Remember Elliott? Elliott's parents were devoutly religious, church-going people. Does that surprise you? Probably not, because you know that Christian parents have shortcomings too. In fact some "good Christian homes" seem to specialize in subtle shaming strategies. Chapter six highlights some of these strategies.

6
Abuse and Shaming by Christian Parents

*C*hristian parents are not perfect parents.

Parents might be Christians, but there might still be dysfunction in a family, because unfortunately, even Christian parents can be consistently inadequate in their parenting. For instance, incest may occur as often in Christian homes as it does in non-Christian homes, according to Christian psychologist Grant Martin.[1]

How can this be if Christians have the Spirit of Truth living in them to show them right from wrong? Alas, it is possible to quench the Spirit. When Christian men and women marry, they establish families that function somewhere between believably biblical and downright pharisaical, often mirroring their own families of origin.

Shaming in Pharisaical Families
The Gospels depict the Pharisees, with few exceptions, as rigidly relig-

ious and without a genuine love for God or faith in his Son. However, I want to suggest that even genuine followers of Jesus Christ can be pharisaical in their approach to living and parenting. If that's true, how would their families function? I believe they would be remarkably like other very dysfunctional families.

The Pharisees were trapped in intergenerational patterns that blinded them to the truth of God. In Mark 7:5 they ask Jesus why his disciples didn't live according "to the tradition of the elders"—a top priority for them. And in verse 13 of that chapter, Jesus told the Pharisees, "Thus you nullify the word of God by your tradition that you have handed down. . . ."

It is possible for Christian parents to perpetuate intergenerational patterns of subtle and even overt abuse as they follow the traditions of *their* abusive parents. In these families, truth is an enemy to sinful traditions, just at it was to the Pharisees. These Christians are experts at distorting the truth to justify their own actions, just as the Pharisees were.

One woman told me that, as he molested her, her father would quote Ephesians 6:1, "Children, obey your parents in the Lord, for this is right." This use of Scripture is a distortion of reality and denial of truth—the hallmarks of dysfunctional families—at their most destructive. Is it any wonder this Christian woman battles daily to escape her shame-based identity? And can you understand why she finds it difficult to trust God?

Appearance Management versus Genuine Repentance

As you might imagine, that abusive father was deeply invested in appearance management, apparently to the complete neglect of genuine repentance. This is also a fundamentally pharisaical approach to life.

Jesus observed in Luke 11:39, "Now then, you Pharisees clean the outside of the cup and dish, but inside you are full of greed and wickedness." This external focus can prevail in fundamentally pharisaical families even when overt abuse never occurs. And it can lead to devastating emotional abuse.

Carolyn's Christian parents greeted the news of her embarrassing pregnancy with personal condemnation and persistent calls for her to get an abortion. " 'We're not about to become the latest grist for the church gossip mill,' my folks told me. I was so ashamed, confused and scared I wanted to die. Instead, I let my baby die so our family wouldn't be embarrassed. I can't forgive them, and I can't forgive myself."

Pleasing People versus Pleasing God

In John 12:43, Jesus pronounces a scathing indictment that summarized the Pharisee's approach to life. Jesus said of the Pharisees, "They loved praise from men more than praise from God."

In pharisaical homes, Christian mothers and fathers focus more on winning approval from people than approval from God. And they teach this people-pleasing lifestyle to their children.

When pleasing people is a higher priority than obeying God, genuinely Christian parents might become emotionally unavailable to their children because they are addicted to evangelical hyperactivity. This is actually a form of "sanctified" workaholism.

And even if the workaholism is not *fully* "sanctified" by practicing it at church, it can be legitimized with an appropriate Bible verse. For example, boss-pleasing Christian workaholics have been known to say something like, "I'm not a workaholic, I'm just a good provider. And that takes working seventy hours a week in this economy. After all, doesn't 1 Timothy 5:8 say that if people won't provide for their families they've denied the faith and are worse than unbelievers?"

These parents don't have enough emotional energy left even to worry about whether or not they are neglecting their children.

Shame-full Christian parents often attempt to satisfy their emotional hunger with the "praise from men" by being at church every time the doors are open. In the midst of their pharisaical frenzy of "churchiness," they simply do not have time for bringing up children "in the training and instruction of the Lord." (See Ephesians 6:4.) At least, not in the instruction of the Lord as Scripture and Son reveal him.

Misrepresenting God: Pharisee versus Father
Even if a family is not formally religious, children are learning about the attributes of God as surely as seminarians. Parents *always* instruct their children about God. As a child's first authority figures, parents represent the character of God, the ultimate authority figure. Unfortunately, impaired parents in dysfunctional families *mis*represent the character of God—even if these parents are Christians.

Someone has observed facetiously that "man makes God in *his* image." And pharisaical Christian parents tend to make God in the image of an angry, rigid, legalistically unforgiving Pharisee. Then they teach that image of God to their children.

What a distortion of the righteous, loving, forgiving Father that Jesus presented as God! Of all the words he could have used to accurately portray God in human terms, Jesus chose to use *father*. We meet this Father-God most intimately in Luke 15:11-31 in the familiar passage commonly called the Parable of the Prodigal Son.

Shaming in "Believably Biblical" Families
All Christian parents do not misrepresent God so obviously as impaired, pharisaical parents. Most Christian husbands and wives strive to establish homes that are based on biblical principles. These Christian families will not use shame-passing purposely to preserve family secrets and control children. But because there aren't any perfect parents, even committed Christian parents teach some things that can confuse and subtly abuse their children.

In her book, *When Helping You Is Hurting Me: Escaping the Messiah Trap*, Carmen Berry suggests that even well-meaning Christian parents can model and teach such a lie. Berry describes the "Messiah Trap" as comprised of two lies: (1) "If I don't do it, it won't get done"; and (2) "Everyone else's needs take priority over mine."[2]

This author describes a woman she calls Diedre who was raised by loving Christian parents who put great emphasis on helping people in need. All the family gatherings centered around helping others, and the children were expected to be unfailingly quiet and giving. Diedre and her siblings learned that their needs were not only unimportant, but were a source of embarrassment and irritation to their parents. These sincere and godly parents inadvertently taught their children that they were responsible for meeting every person's every need while totally ignoring their own legitimate needs.

Berry concludes that even Christian adults who remember their childhoods as "happy" can be caught in the painful "Messiah Trap."

Diedre struggled as she came to see how her godly, well-meaning parents had presented her with a distorted view of love, God and of her place in the world. She had been a "good" girl, which, in essence, meant that she had no opportunity to be a girl at all. . . . Like Diedre, many Messiahs . . . choose to pretend to have a happy childhood when in fact they had little, if any, childhood at all.[3]

Diedre was not a victim of overt abuse at the hands of profoundly impaired parents. But she had been taught some lies that led her to adopt a lifestyle marked by disrespectful, rescuing relationships.

Like Diedre, you might have been raised in a home with genuinely godly parents. Nevertheless, you need to be open to recognizing the lies you learned, no matter how well-intentioned their source.

Even well-meaning Christian parents are not perfect people. They could not give you what they never received. They probably raised you in much the same way they were raised, so you will need to look at your parents' parents to get a wider, clearer view of your past.

Jennifer, a lovely Christian woman in her thirties, was thoroughly confused about why a best-selling paperback on the topic of adult children of alcoholics seemed to describe her life so well. To her counselor's question about parental alcoholism, Jennifer incredulously replied, "My folks were good, teetotaling Southern Baptists. I think I must be nuts."

But as she explored her family history, Jennifer remembered that both her grandfathers were alcoholics. As Christians, her parents were obsessed with avoiding "the curse of drunkenness" in their children. Jennifer recalled that they always checked her breath when she returned from dates.

"My mom and dad owned a small bookstore, and it was not unusual for both of them to work sixty or seventy hours a week. They were so exhausted when they came home that they had no energy left for me and my younger brother. Dad was always dozing off or staring blankly at the TV, and Mom was perpetually angry at him, us kids and at life in general."

Jennifer took over almost total care of the home and her younger brother by the time she was ten years old. Clearly, Jennifer's folks, raised by alcoholic and co-alcoholic parents, had reproduced the *dynamics* of an alcoholic family without the alcohol.

As did Jennifer's parents, your parents probably did the best they knew—not the best they *could*, but the best they *knew*. Even if they *cared* enough to do a better job of parenting, *knowing how* is the crucial factor. And, even if they had known how to do better, they could not completely have met all of your needs.

Honoring Your "Heavy" Parents

I suspect some of you are feeling awfully uncomfortable by now because you believe you are dishonoring your folks when you examine their parenting styles. You might be especially uncomfortable if you know they are sincere Christians.

In Exodus 20:12, God instructs us to "honor" our fathers and mothers. In the original language, the word for honor literally meant to be heavy. Eventually it meant to consider persons weighty, important or honorable, as in the case of city officials.[4]

With that word picture in view, it seems to me that we are honoring our parents when we consider their heavy influences in our lives. To ignore the weight of their examples and influences would be dishonoring our parents.

Time Out

Perhaps you actually have been dishonoring your parents by trying to live as though they have had no effect on your life. Pause right now and ask God to help you begin to honor your parents by honestly assessing the weight of their influences. It might be easier to do this if you try to realize that no matter what you remember and learn about the level of abuse in your childhood, God will give you the grace to face it, feel it and forgive it.

Personal Reflection
☐ List the attributes of the father described in Luke 15:11-31.

☐ Did you notice that the son expected a cold shoulder from his father but received the father's warm embrace instead? He didn't have to be persuaded against his will to grudgingly tolerate the wayward lad. This father has a heart bent toward forgiving.

☐ Is that how *you* see God?

Looking Ahead
As you have looked more closely at your childhood and at your parents' "heavy" impact on your life, you might be feeling profoundly weighed down with years of accumulated pain. What's the connection?

In chapter seven, we will examine the process by which parental acts and attitudes can become stumbling blocks that cause deep spiritual, personal and interpersonal wounds.

7

Understanding Consequences and Change

W ith the first sins of the first parents, *Adam* and *Eve, a chain reaction* of imperfect parenting and denial of truth began. An unbroken chain of brokenness spans the centuries as each succeeding generation of children lives with the falsehoods of their parents and their parents' parents before them.

As noted in chapter two, the cause of binding shame is an interaction of these falsehoods, the magical thinking of children and the need for a protective illusion of control. The consequences are great.

In my life, binding shame produced all the traits you will read about in this chapter. As you read, look for them in your own life. Chapters eight through eleven well present a more detailed description of these major consequences of binding shame.

Existence Guilt, Abandonment and Perfectionism

Existence guilt says, "I don't deserve to take up space on this planet, and I feel guilty for existing." This makes a lot of sense if I see myself as having a hideous and unique birth defect—an invisible *identity* defect.

And no wonder I *fear* abandonment! I believe I *deserve* abandonment for being so fatally flawed by imperfection.

Now here's the tricky part! How am I ever going to keep perfect people around me? Won't they abandon me the instant they recognize that I am grotesquely unlike them? Is there any hope of maintaining relationships with these people? Of course there is! And we figured it out years ago. *We have to pretend to be perfect too.*

What a brilliant solution! What a clever strategy! And what an exhausting charade! Pretending to be perfect guarantees failure, disappointment and self-shaming.

Self-shaming

As night follows day, self-shaming follows attempts to be perfect, because we never make it. Self-shaming is expressed by inner-commentaries on our consistent failures. These internal, inaudible commentaries originate in the verbal and nonverbal identity statements parents send their children.

Eventually, parents' "you are" statements to children become internalized as "I am" identity concepts. For example, if you heard your parents say, "You are such a dummy!" when you made mistakes as a child, you will probably hear yourself saying, "I am such a dummy!" when you make mistakes now.

Self-shaming is also displayed in many forms of self-neglect and abuse. These forms include poor physical care and even self-mutilation, and they could represent subtle, perhaps subliminal, suicide. Suicide, in any form, expresses a sense of hopelessness and the failure of self-protective defenses.

Hopelessness and Self-protection

In some profoundly painful way, shame-bound "caterpillars" believe they will *never* fly across the chasm separating them from the "butterflies" on the other side.

And if you are the world's only caterpillar, you can't risk revealing that you are an imperfect "bogus butterfly." So your safest stance is self-protection. This brings us full circle because perfectionism is often the chosen means of self-protection.

This painful cycle of shame continues, gaining momentum with each passing day. You might be in misery, feeling that you will never escape from its destructive pattern. It's not unusual for adult children from dysfunctional families to feel overwhelmed with a sense of personal brokenness when they first face the effects of their binding shame. I did. I felt like a crumpled, crippled heap of humanity. Maybe you see yourself the same way.

I have good news for both of us. We do not have to *remain* broken. And if we do, we—not our parents—are responsible for that choice.

Recovery and Responsibility

We've seen that those of us raised in dysfunctional families have traits that cause significant personal and interpersonal problems in our lives. These unhealthy characteristics are an interaction of our sin natures; our brokenness in thinking, feeling and relating which resulted from being caused to stumble as children; and our subsequent sinful and self-protective choices. And although we aren't responsible for being taught lies as children, we are responsible as adults to enter a lifelong process of recovering from the brokenness that the lies caused.

The alternative is to pass the intergenerational baton of brokenness and shame to our offspring just as *our* parents passed it from *their* parents to us. This alternative is the antithesis of the transformation process God plans for us through the renewing of our minds.

Recovering from the effects of growing up in a dysfunctional family can be a difficult, slow and painful process. Remember, Christ can supervise your rehabilitation and recovering process. Depending on the severity of your personal brokenness and the extent of your cooperation with the work of his Spirit in your life, you will be able to "soar

on wings like eagles, . . . run and not grow weary . . . [or at least] walk
and not be faint" (Isaiah 40:31).
I am in this recovering process and always will be. It is hard, hum-
bling work. But I am happy to report that there are fewer "fainting"
days and more "running" and "soaring" days than there used to be. And
I've learned that living in the recovering process means traveling a new
path and following a new map.

Following a New Map
I recently read one of the more amusing revelations from post-*glasnost*
Russia. It seems the chief of the principal mapping agency admitted
that for the last fifty years Soviet mapmakers deliberately misplaced
rivers and streets, distorted boundaries and omitted geographical fea-
tures on public maps. The article went on to say that correct maps were
still "top secret" in the Soviet Union long after space photography
allowed foreign countries to make their own extremely accurate maps.
"People did not recognize their motherland on maps. Tourists tried
in vain to orient themselves on the terrain. . . . You can get maps of
our country in many countries of the world except for the U.S.S.R.,"
the [Moscow] evening paper . . . complained recently. "From whom,
one wonders, are we keeping secrets? From ourselves?"[1]
That's a good question—one you might want to ask yourself. Dysfunctional families are famous for keeping secrets from themselves. And as
a loyal child, you might still be trying in vain to orient yourself to life
with a parent-drawn map of secrets and lies.
No wonder you've lost your way and feel confused. You need to
begin following a new map charted by truth. But that won't be easy
because in dysfunctional families, truth brings pain.

Committing to Truth
It has been said that truth makes you free but first it makes you miserable. I have experienced this principle in action. It was very painful
to accept and work through the memories of being molested. But that
childhood truth clarified important issues in my adult life. And I have

seen freeing truth bring temporary pain in the lives of many others.

If we run from truth we will continue to wander through life following a map marked with distortion and denial. As children, we might have been taught to turn away from truth and evade it. Recovering from binding shame begins when we turn *toward* truth and *embrace* it—truth about our families and truth about ourselves.

☐ *Commit yourself to truth about family influences and control.* I have challenged you repeatedly to consider the truth about your family's influences on your life. With all this emphasis on the power of parental and familial influences, you must not miss this life-changing truth: influence is *not* control.

Your past influences you, but your past does not have to control you.

Burn that sentence into your mind. Its truth springs the cage door of hopelessness and frees you to pursue the truth about your right to choose and change.

☐ *Commit yourself to truth about personal choices and change.* You are no longer the powerless victim of others' choices. As an adult, you are now a purposeful agent with choices of your own. You do not have to continue heedlessly recreating the destructive patterns you observed and then absorbed in your childhood. You can change.

That promise might sound as impossible to you as it did at first to Penny. Raised by verbally and emotionally abusive parents, Penny was convinced that she was totally worthless.

"I can't tell you the number of times I heard them say I wasn't worth the salt in a biscuit," she said.

As Penny learned about choices and changes possible in the recovering process, she was amazed.

"I can't tell you what a mind-blowing concept that was for me."

Penny's eyes gleamed with excitement and tears as she described her response to the concept of making new choices. "Honestly, I've always believed I was destined to be a miserable misfit my entire life. It never occurred to me that my past had any relationship to my life today. I always thought, 'Oh well, that's just the way I am.' And I never dared dream about maybe being different in the future. I just never knew I had choices about how to live my life. Wow, that changes everything. Doesn't it?"

Yes, it does. It did for Penny, and it can for you.

An ancient Chinese proverb states: "If we do not change our direction, we are likely to end up where we are headed." You *can* change your direction. It will mean following a new, truth-oriented map to chart a course for change.

What we live with, we learn, and what we learn, we practice. What we practice, we become, and what we become has consequences.[2] You lived with shaming; you learned binding shame. You have practiced shaming yourself and others, and your life has become shame-full.

The remainder of this book focuses on new choices for changing shame-bound areas of your life. There will be opportunities to learn new truths, and you will be invited to practice some new choices. Why not start now?

Personal Reflection

☐ Here is one of the most important choices: Begin to notice the "shaming committee" inside your head. Perhaps your parents are the chairpersons, but there are additional members, such as siblings, teachers, etc. You hear their critical commentaries whenever you fail to measure up to their "shoulds" and "oughts."

☐ Think of some circumstances during this past week when you experienced shame because you made mistakes. What commentaries did you hear? (Perhaps you also recalled a shaming scene from childhood. If so, describe that. Our shame-generating commentaries seem to be more like mental video tapes than audio tapes.)

Circumstance	*Shame-based Commentary/Scene*
You leave your briefcase at the office or forget to buy an ingredient you need for a recipe.	"You are so stupid and forgetful. Can't you do anything right?" (I see myself as a kid forgetting my schoolbooks.)

☐ Now, look at those circumstances again. How would the commentary be different if it were based upon the truth of your imperfection and human limitations? (For example: "I forgot something," instead of, "I'm so stupid.")

☐ Here's an important truth. God knows you better than anyone in the universe—warts and all—yet values you. God's opinion of you is based on the truth of your imperfection and human limitations, and all the while he cherishes you. Jesus knew you were an imperfect sinner. It was such an important fact to him that he chose to die in your place.

☐ *The best choice you will ever make is asking Jesus into your life.* You can do that right now if you sincerely want to be forgiven and become part of God's family. You can pray something like this:

Dear God, I know that I have sinned and am cut off from you. Thank you for providing the payment for my sin and a way into your family. I believe that Jesus died for my sins, and I accept him right now as my own personal Savior and Lord. Lord Jesus, please come into my life and make me all you want me to be. Thank you for promising that you would. Amen.

☐ If you are a brand new member of God's family, here are some options that will pay rich dividends in your life if you choose to do them. If you have been a Christian for some time, check off the options you've already chosen to do consistently (not perfectly). If you don't practice some, then consider noting when and how you will begin.

_____ 1. Get a Bible in a translation you can understand easily. Select one that has information to help you study and understand Scripture.
When and how I will do this:

_____ 2. Join a church that teaches the Bible and demonstrates God's love and grace. (Please don't try to "go it alone." God never intended you to be a spiritual "Lone Ranger.")
When and how I will do this:

_____ 3. Set aside time each day to talk to God and to listen to him as he "speaks" from the Bible.

When and how I will do this:

_____ 4. Find a Christian (of the same sex) or a small group of Christians (can be co-ed) with whom you can meet regularly for support and encouragement. Spending part of the time in Bible study is valuable. (Remember, spiritual mentors aren't perfect people. So Scripture, not the opinions of others, must be your guide.)

When and how I will do this:

Looking Ahead

In his best-selling book, *Healing for Damaged Emotions,* David Seamands tells this story about Henry Ford and the electronics genius Charlie Steinmetz, who designed the huge generators for Ford's first plant. When one of those crucial generators broke down and the assembly line came to a screeching halt, Ford called Steinmetz. He came out and spent a few hours puttering around with some gauges. When he finished, Steinmetz threw the switch, and the plant was back in business.

Several days later, Ford received a bill for $10,000. Surprised at the amount, he returned the bill with a note asking Steinmetz if he didn't agree that that was a very high price for a "few hours of tinkering around on those motors."

This time, Steinmetz sent Ford an *itemized* bill which read:

For Tinkering Around on the Motors:	$ 10
For Knowing *Where* to Tinker:	9,990
Total:	$10,000

Ford paid the bill.[3]

Perhaps you are reading this book partly because you sense that your *life* has "broken down" in some important areas. If you are a Christian, you have the presence of God, the Holy Spirit, dwelling within you.

And, believe me, God knows precisely where to tinker. As you read, ask God to tinker exactly where you need fixing.

Why not take a moment to do that right now before we look at how to be released from shaming our flaws?

8
Released from Shaming Our Flaws

T*he story goes that a man was driving on a country road when a woman* approached from the other direction. As she got near him, she rolled down her window, stuck out her head and began screaming, "Pig! Pig!"

Now this guy was tired of all the women's-lib rhetoric describing men with that unflattering term, so he yelled back furiously, "Sow! Sow!" Pleased with his rapid retort, he rounded a curve and promptly plowed into a pig in the middle of the road.

Like the man in my story, if we interpret every interaction as a commentary on our identities, we are apt to run into big trouble.

The Self-Shaming/Self-Focus Connection
As I observe the shame-bound lives of most adult children from dysfunctional families, I am struck by our self-focused perspectives. We

tend to go through life in self-protective postures, scrutinizing all interactions to determine what they say about us. And this is as true of
shame-bound Christians as it is of unbelievers.

The difference is that many sincere Christians are unknowingly self-
focused on not *appearing* self-focused. In fact, the whole idea of examining our self-concepts appears very "unspiritual" to them. If you are
one of these folks, and if you are from a shame-bound, dysfunctional
family, the chances are good that you are living a self-focused and self-
shaming existence without even knowing it. I invite you to openly
acknowledge your imperfection, your sense of being different and deficient, your self-shaming and your defensive self-focus. This is a prerequisite to making new choices. Certainly it was for me.

Without realizing it, I lived most of my life making choices based
on shame and self-protection. I didn't begin to make new choices and
change until I saw, understood and owned the earlier choices.

Perhaps you've heard that "you can't heal it if you don't feel it." I'm
suggesting that *you can't free it if you don't see it.* You cannot be free of
your self-shaming until you knowingly choose to adopt a purposeful,
temporary self-focus. I'm not saying we should spend our lives in in-
trospective "navel gazing." We look *within* for the same reason we look
back—to provide a context for change. In reality, our shame-bound self-
concepts affect us and our relationships with God and others whether
we know it or not. When we recognize these effects, we can make new
choices for changing the old, self-protective patterns into more fulfilling and Christ-honoring ones.

Time Out

As an adult child from a dysfunctional family, you probably have
developed destructive and defensive patterns of living which include
unconscious self-shaming and self-focusing. Take a moment to consider some evidence of this in your own life.

For instance:

☐ Are you so uncomfortable when you receive compliments about your appearance or achievements that you try to deny or diminish them?

☐ Do you spend less mental energy listening to others than you do preparing your rebuttal?

☐ Do you think it is a sign of weakness to ask for assistance or directions?

Ask God to give you "wisdom in the hidden parts" of your self-concept so you can recognize the negative effects of believing that others are perfect but you're not. Then ask him to help you learn to see yourself as *he* sees you.

Why is it so difficult for many adult children from dysfunctional families to choose a purposeful, temporary self-focus? *Because one of the dysfunctional family's most powerful, shaming legacies is the belief that any attention to yourself is wrong or sinful.* This is just one of the connections between binding shame we learned as children and self-shaming we practice as adults.

The Binding Shame/Self-Shaming Connection

Binding shame puts us eternally on trial, and the verdict is always *guilty*. Self-shaming administers punishment for the crime of imperfection, and the sentence is either the death penalty or life imprisonment. In the most tragic cases, the sentence is executed by suicide. More frequently, we imprison ourselves in dungeons of self-hatred and hopelessness.

We each have flaws—imperfections and limitations in our perceptions, our intellects, our skills and our physical strength. Do these natural, human flaws embarrass you? Mine do. I've already admitted that this is an area where I continue to struggle. Let's take a closer look at why we feel ashamed of these limitations.

Shaming Our Perceptions, Intellects and Skills

We misperceive situations sometimes, but basically our perceptions are as sound as anyone else's. We don't know and understand *every*thing, but we know and understand *many* things. Why do adult children have a hard time believing that? Why have many clinicians and authors noted a kind of mental confusion in most adult children? Jennifer's story offers a clue.

"It was so weird. I still feel confused when I think about it or talk about it." Jennifer's pretty face twisted into a perplexed expression and she gazed off into an unseen fog. "My stepdad liked to get me down on the floor and tickle me all the time. But when my mom wasn't home, his tickling was different. I remember so clearly the first time he pulled down my pants and stuck his fingers in my vagina."

Jennifer paused and looked into my eyes as if searching for confirmation that such things happen. "I was so surprised and so scared I just went numb. After a couple minutes, I jumped up and said, 'Why did you do that?' He said, 'Do what?' I thought I must have imagined it all. I mean, I thought I was crazy. He said I was acting crazy. I guess it sounds silly, but I wanted to talk to someone about it just to see if they had ever heard of that happening before. But I was too ashamed to tell anyone. Besides, I think maybe I was afraid of what they'd say, afraid he was right about me being crazy."

Jennifer's feeling that she was crazy has extended into her young-adult life. She deeply distrusts her own perceptions.

Variations on the theme of "craziness" occur in most dysfunctional families, and they have similar effects. If you are one of the adult children who lived with craziness, you might be shaming yourself for being crazy instead of recognizing that you were raised in a "crazy-making" family.

In addition to feeling crazy, you might also feel stupid. This view of yourself has much less to do with your intellect and skills than with the information and skill *gaps* experienced by most adult children.

Something Missing

Memory gaps refer to information or experiences you had as a child but conveniently forgot in order to benefit the family system. There are other types of gaps as well. Information and skill gaps exist because your parents were too distressed and distracted to provide some of the basic knowledge and experiences supplied to children in well-functioning homes. For example, competent parents teach and model such things as problem solving, basic nutrition and appropriate social behavior. In dysfunctional homes, children are supposed simply to know these things without having been taught. As small adults, they are expected to organize a term paper, cook or resolve conflict correctly the first time around. In consistently adequate families, such things are learned.

You might be shaming yourself for being stupid when in reality you are very bright and creative. What you are labeling as stupidity is actually the sense of confusion commonly experienced by adults who never had the opportunity as children to learn and try lots of basic things. And if you've never stopped to look at your family and its problems, you wouldn't have seen all the learning experiences you missed as a child. You have just always assumed there was something missing in *you*.

In chapter four, I suggested that the "be blind" rule in dysfunctional families teaches young children to devalue and disown their perceptions, and later in life to seek external validation of their opinions and decisions. They become easy targets for those secular and religious "experts" who amass fabulous fortunes and/or faithful followings by proclaiming *their* personal perceptions as the ultimate answers to all the questions of life. When Christian adult children flock after ecclesiastical gurus, they become less and less disciples of the Lord and more and more disciples of disciples. It probably is true that most Christian leaders find themselves thrust into a guru role they never sought. However, it is also true that Christians leaders are still sinners just like us. The unquestioning adoration of a faithful flock might blind some of them to the dangers of the guru role.

Shaming Our Physical Limitations

Obviously, shaming our perceptions, intellect and skills can cause problems. But shaming our appropriate human limitations of physical strength and endurance can cause injury, illness and even death.[1]

Maybe this topic calls up visions of a burly adult child trying to impress his wife or girlfriend by moving a piano singlehandedly or playing hours of killer racketball without losing or resting. If so, be assured that I've seen "ninety-pound weaklings" push past their appropriate human limitations too. One forty-year-old woman stayed up all night before college finals and then skipped breakfast to go directly to her eight-hour shift in a factory after finishing the exams. (By the way, the piano mover referred to himself as a wimp when he strained some muscles, and the sleepless student was angry with herself for dozing off on the job.)

Or what about the many adult children who consistently defy medical and nutritional guidelines for healthful living? All these people live as if their bodies possess no limitations and require no care. Do you live that way?

I'm well aware that we human beings are capable of amazing physical feats. I've seen several world swimming records set. I agree that it *is* phenomenal what dedicated, disciplined athletes can accomplish. But even Mark Spitz requires sleep—indeed his longevity as an athelete is the result of respecting his body's needs!

Having physical limitations does not mean we are weak or wimpy. It means we are human. By all means, be the best you can be physically, but don't shame yourself for falling short of your goals. If you are an adult child, the chances are strong that your goals might be somewhat unrealistic anyway. Unfortunately, because most adult children tend to think in the dichotomous absolutes of "all-or-nothing," anything less than meeting *all* your goals might seem like total failure. This belief is the bedrock of perfectionism. And perfectionism is the mask we wear to hide our human limitations.

The Mask of Perfectionism
Most adult children from dysfunctional families conclude early in life that it is dangerous to let the *real* mistake-making you show. So we

fashioned disguises, masks of perfection. These masks are extremely cumbersome and ill-fitting. We get *so* exhausted holding them in place. I know that I did! Besides, they constrict and chafe, since they weren't designed to fit *real* imperfect people like you and me.

Perfectionism is an unhealthy pattern of thoughts and behaviors we use to conceal our flaws. Perfectionism also serves to compensate for a poor self-concept and the painful sense of binding shame underlying it.

Perfectionism has two dimensions, relational and personal. On the relational level, perfectionism is intended to conceal our flaws from others. This becomes a matter of life and death if we believe our imperfections isolate us from the rest of perfect humanity.

On the personal plane, perfectionism serves to *compensate* rather than conceal. If you are committed to a perfectionistic lifestyle, you already know the "awful truth" about your limitations. Your only hope is to compensate for some of the pain you feel by gaining the praise and prominence won through perfectionistic pleasing and performing.

Rookie perfectionists can be spotted pretty quickly. They have to be the best at *everything* they do at work or play.

Did I say play? What a joke! There is no such thing as play for a hardcore, rookie perfectionist. *Everything* is a life-or-death, must-win situation. Rookies demand spotlessness and order of themselves and others *everywhere*—the desks at work, the kitchen cupboards at home, etc., *ad insufferable*.

I have a friend who was a rookie perfectionist years ago. She kept her home, herself and her children spotless. She even dressed her little boys in white shoes all the time! And since she saw scuff marks as moral failings, she polished those little white shoes every day—even on camping trips! Of course back then I was a rookie perfectionist too so I didn't think that was particularly strange. (We perfectionists adore being together because we validate each other's compulsions.)

Both of us are more sophisticated these days. And many of us who have been at this performing and pleasing business a little longer know too much to want to *look* perfectionistic! In fact, the primary way you know you have graduated from rookie to veteran perfectionist status is that you want to be perfect at not looking perfectionistic!

Die-hard perfectionists are always quicker to relinquish perfectionistic *behavior* than perfectionistic *beliefs*. But only the latter leads to genuine change. Anything less just prolongs the inevitable problems that perfectionism brings.

Problems and Perks of Perfectionism

When we can't distinguish between a commitment to excellence and pathological perfectionism, we create problems in our lives. No matter what we do, it's not good enough. We fear failing in *any* area of life. When we do inevitably fail, the resulting self-criticism leads to loss of self-esteem. This often triggers episodes of depression. As perfectionists, we can't tolerate criticism from others in any form, so we react defensively and alienate those close to us. This only reinforces our belief that we must be perfect to be accepted and loved.

With problems related to work efficiency, emotional stability and relational harmony, why would perfectionists be as resistant to change as many counselors report? What are the fringe benefits reinforcing perfectionism?

Perfectionists are often rewarded for their life-crushing compulsion. This is as true in the church as it is in the office—if not more so. Christians call it determination or dedication or a dozen other euphemisms that camouflage perfectionism's self-protective, shame-based origins. The euphemisms focus on positive pay-offs such as success and visibility in the company, the church or the community. We tend to forget that perfectionism by any name still is shame-based bondage and denial of truth.

Perfectionism is a rejection of biblical truth about our sin-brokenness. We are creatures with enormous, but not unbounded, potential. But this is not good enough if we believe that achieving perfection is our only ticket across the broken relational bridge to the mythical perfect people on the other side. And even if we achieve high goals, we might still feel ineligible for success and acceptance. We might look like butterflies to others but *we* know we are really just caterpillars. Fortunately, no one else has noticed—*yet*.

Yet. That's the operative word for all the hardworking, successful, shame-bound perfectionists who live the Imposter Phenomenon. The Imposter Phenomenon is the name given to the experience of individuals who have the uneasy feeling that if they achieved something of significance, they really just "faked" their way through it. What's more, everyone is going to spot them as inadequate and unworthy imposters at any moment.

I am intimately acquainted with the Imposter Phenomenon, and so are millions of other adult children from dysfunctional families, including Brent.

As a child, Brent's emotionally absent father and his perfectionistic mother convinced him that he was unimportant and inadequate. Brent had never heard of the Imposter Phenomenon, but he has lived it for many years.

Brent was embarrassed to admit it even to me, but he thinks he's a fake. He holds a key position with a national ministry, and people all over the country look to him for leadership and creative ideas. What's more, they aren't disappointed with what Brent offers them. But Brent hasn't taken a vacation in six years because he's afraid that if he leaves even for a week it will become obvious that he doesn't really *do* anything. Every time he gets an official-looking letter from ministry headquarters, he's afraid he's going to be fired for incompetence. Brent's wife and children receive little of his time, and Brent has a massive case of burn-out—even though Brent gives seminars on how to avoid burn-out. This only comfirms to Brent that he's a fake.

Like many Christian adult children in church and parachurch ministries, Brent feels like an imposter because he struggles to match his walk with his talk. Brent allows himself to be overworked and overwhelmed. Brent needs to look at himself and say, "My limitations don't disqualify me from the human race, they validate my entry form!"

Perfectionism is a bottomless pit of demands and disappointments because you can *never* satisfy its specifications. Even if you get close in *one* part of your life, you will be left to face all those other messy, imperfect areas. No wonder you exhaust yourself performing as you try to jump through hoops you or others hold ever higher and higher.

Would you like to retire the hoops and be released from the bondage of perfectionism? Believe me, the sense of relief and freedom that this would bring is worth whatever it takes to change. But change is a process of making new choices.

New Choices and Truth

I recently heard about an executive plagued by a strange malady that caused splitting headaches and ringing in his ears. He first went to an ear, nose and throat specialist who corrected his deviated septum, but the condition grew worse. He consulted an opthamologist who performed delicate optic nerve surgery, and, later, a dentist did a root canal. Still he had no relief. He finally sought a world-famous brain surgeon who said the only other case he'd seen like that had been fatal within a year.

This man was despondent. He decided to quit his high-paying job and spend his retirement money on whatever he wanted. He had always longed to indulge himself with custom-made shirts and suits, so the first thing he did was find a top-rated tailor. As the tailor was measuring him for shirts, he called out the numbers to an assistant. "Sleeve: thirty-five inches. Neck: sixteen-and-a-half inches."

"Oh, no," said the executive. "I've always worn a fifteen-inch collar. You'd better check again."

The tailor did, and again measured sixteen-and-a-half inches.

"But I insist you make it fifteen inches, because that's what I've always worn."

"Okay," said the tailor, "but don't blame me if you get splitting headaches and ringing in your ears!"

Isn't it strange that we seek the solution to our personal pain everywhere but from God, who has the answer? Certainly this is the case when it comes to relieving the pain that shame-based perfectionism inflicts.

Believing and acting on truth will release our suffering executive from pain. And choosing, thinking and living truth brings release from the bondage of looking with shame on our human flaws and limitations. Let's look at three specific areas where applied truth will set us free from self-shaming: truth about imperfection, perceptions and self-care.

Truth about Perfection

The butterfly lie promotes the fantasy that this is a perfect world populated by perfect people and that since I am not perfect I don't belong. Biblical truth proclaims the fact that this is a broken world, filled with imperfect and sinful people, and since I am imperfect and sinful too I fit right in.

Inherent in our sin natures is a deep sense that something in us is missing or not quite right. Instead of accepting God's way to deal with this accurate perception of our sin-broken imperfection, Romans 1:25 says we "exchanged the truth of God for a lie." We attempted to create our own self-righteous solution. (See Romans 3:9-28.)

The first few chapters of Romans portray us as sinful beings who turn away from the truth about ourselves, about God and about God's remedy for our brokenness. This truth includes some liberating paradoxes about our worth and God's grace. Release from feeling shame over our imperfections is found in embracing these liberating paradoxes.

☐ *We must accept the liberating paradox of our worth.* At the most elemental levels of our identities, *we are unworthy but not worthless.* This is true whether or not a person is a Christian.

I find that people struggle with that concept from one of two perspectives. Some are highly indignant at the suggestion that they are unworthy in any way whatsoever. Others sincerely believe that they are utterly worthless blobs—human worms. Either way, their conclusions are based on their own imperfect perceptions of themselves which have been shaped by the imperfect perceptions of others.

You and I, as created beings, spend a lot of time and energy trying to figure out who we are. Meanwhile, our Creator has the truth. We find his answer in the cross and the liberating paradox it represents: We are unworthy but not worthless.

□ *We must accept the liberating paradox of God's grace.* Most of us work hard to conceal the fact that there is anything wrong with us. In contrast, God's grace reflects a liberating paradox: When we acknowledge ourselves as all wrong, God acknowledges us as all right. When we admit our sinful imperfection and trust in Jesus, we receive God's grace. That's why "good people" reject God's way of grace. Grace forces "good people" to own their badness. Embracing this liberating paradox releases us from biblical and binding shame. It shatters the chains that keep us from being all God plans for us. And a third liberating paradox opens the door to God's planned potential in our lives.

□ *We must accept the liberating paradox of potential.* Perfectionism paralyzes. Embracing your *limited* potential paradoxically frees you to achieve *more* of your potential. Accepting the truth that neither you nor anyone else is perfect liberates you to dream, risk, dare and be more than you ever could if shackled by the straightjacket of perfectionism.

I know! I did not want my first book to be good, I wanted it to be *perfect.* And that desire for perfection almost prevented it from being at all. I was paralyzed until I faced my perfectionistic compulsion and made some new choices. When I began, I wanted every chapter to be the finest and most complete treatment of the topic ever written. That changed to a deep desire for a thorough, skillful and sensitive presentation of the material. Sometimes the difference between perfectionism and a commitment to excellence is difficult to explain. For me, it meant coming to the point of saying, "That's really quite good. Not perfect, but good enough." This is an enormously liberating approach to life. Believe me!

You don't need to fear imperfection, because it does not reveal your unacceptable difference from other humans. It reveals you *are* human. That goes for your perceptions too. As one among a planetful of imperfect humans, you have perceptions that are potentially as accurate as anyone else's.

Truth about Perceptions

When we learn more about the dynamics of functional and dysfunctional families, we perceive our childhood experiences more accurately. This is an important element in our recovering processes as adult children from a dysfunctional families. Additionally, as we understand the effects of those childhood experiences, we will better understand our current choices and relationships.

Even when we read books, attend groups and do the other things that help us replace lies with the truth, we might tend to give away our opinions and discount our perceptions too easily.

If we doubt our own capacity to reach valid opinions, we might be startled to learn that we can hear God speak to us directly through his Word with his Spirit as our teacher. (See 1 John 2:27.) Equally amazing is the fact that God invites us to speak to him directly to receive help and wisdom. (See Hebrews 4:16 and James 1:5 for examples.)

Driving home from work one evening, a commuter was horrified to realize that the engine of his car was on fire. He pulled off the road, leaped out the door and watched while his car was completely gutted in a few minutes. Later he remembered that he had a fire extinguisher in the trunk but had forgotten about it in, dare I say, the *heat* of the moment.

This commuter possessed a resource that would have reduced the damage to his car significantly if he had used it. We Christians possess a far more powerful resource in the indwelling Holy Spirit. Unfortunately, that resource all too often goes unused by many of us who desperately need guidance and wisdom to prevent burn-out in our lives.

What would it mean if we began to make new choices, shame-free choices, founded on the truth that our limited capacity to understand God's truth is not greater or less than anyone else's limited capacity? We might have to put away all those great tapes and pull out God's book to study for ourselves.

One thing that God's Word tells us is that God wants you to care for your body as if it was his—because it is! Yet we adult children tend to ignore our physical needs. We need to know the truth about these needs.

Truth about Self-care

Self-care encompasses such obvious elements as refusing to tolerate abuse, but it also includes giving adequate attention to proper exercise and nutrition. Self-care is influenced by cultural, as well as family, patterns, and this is a "double-whammy" for adult children in this country.

Studies estimate that the average American consumes about 125 pounds of sugar and 22 pounds of chemicals each year.[2] Apparently, many of us treat our bodies more like toxic dump sites than temples of the Holy Spirit.

And according to Christian physician Keith Sehnert,

Recent reports have indicated that more than 90 percent of the ailments we suffer, we have brought upon ourselves. Thus the most significant impact on the health of Americans will not come from an increase in funds for acute care medicine, but from the impact of individual changes in lifestyle.[3]

Positive changes in eating and exercise habits are difficult for anyone in this culture. This is true particularly for adult children who grew up in dysfunctional families. We have seen already that we live what we learn. And many adult children repeat the unhealthy and unbiblical lifestyles that were modeled by their impaired parents. These might include irregular eating habits, constant dieting, and inadequate exercise and relaxation time. This is often coupled with too much stress and the consumption of caffeine, tobacco, alcohol and other drugs.

What must we do to make healthier choices to treat our bodies with respect? First, we must give ourselves permission to have legitimate physical needs for adequate rest and self-care. In Mark 6:31 we see Jesus leaving the pressing crowd to get some food and rest, and we see him instructing his disciples to do the same. Jesus teaches us to recognize our physical limitations and meet our self-care needs.

That is quite a contrast from the executive I heard about recently.

This adult child of an alcoholic was so overwhelmed and stressed-out from his demanding job that he said there was no way he could take time to go to a stress-management seminar his company offered.

To make healthier self-care choices, we also need information about nutrition and the benefits of regular excercise. In addition, we must know something about the process of change because wanting a quick-fix will sabotage our health-giving choices.

You are not apt to completely revolutionize your lifestyle by next week. But you can take some steps toward more healthful living. For instance, you could get help to stop smoking. You could give up caffeine, drink more water, reduce your consumption of sugar and fat, and/or eat more fresh fruits and vegetables. Why not select *one* of these suggestions and start improving your self-care?

You don't have to join an expensive fitness center to increase your exercise. Try walking for thirty minutes three times a week. Start slowly and increase your pace gradually. Walking, like any aerobic exercise, will strengthen your heart and bones and speed up your metabolism to help you burn calories more efficiently. It also seems to release chemical messengers in your brain that work as antidepressants. I love the natural high and increased energy that brisk walking produces. And I can tell the difference when I don't walk regularly.

Obviously, if you are quite overweight, very sedentary, and/or have any health problems, you must check with your physician before making even these small lifestyle changes. And please remember, the goal is not a thirty-inch waist for every man or size six shape for every woman. The issue here is health-giving and respectful care for our bodies. For Christians, this issue has a biblical mandate since our bodies are bought with a price and belong to God.

Sometimes we Christians use our desire to "avoid vanity" as a reason to remain overweight and underexercised. Perhaps this choice is shaped more by shame than spirituality. Many Christian adult children might unknowingly take this approach because it allows them to hate themselves for dishonoring their bodies. This reinforces their shame-bound self-concepts that they are different from others. Clearly, this shame-based thinking points out that healthy behavioral choices must grow out of the truth.

Personal Reflection

Recovering from perfectionistic thinking and behaving is a process of continually making new choices based on truth. The truth indeed sets you free from the oppressing burden of trying to live up to impossibly high, self-imposed standards.

☐ Can you think of a current project in which you sense you might be paralyzed by perfectionism? What would an achievable level of excellence for that project? Would you be willing to commit to achievable excellence as being good enough on this project? Why or why not?

☐ If you don't have any aids that teach the basics of Bible study, are you willing to buy at least one? If so, when? (You could ask your pastor for suggestions.)

☐ Which physical self-care habit will you begin? When? (Reread the suggestions just presented for some options to choose from.)

☐ Appendix B contains Scripture verses that tell us how God sees his children. Will you use these verses to begin learning to see yourself as God sees you? When?

Looking Ahead

Perfectionism is conceived in emotional pain and gives birth "after its own kind." This is a serious dilemma if we are adult children from dysfunctional families because we are uncomfortable with emotions—*any* emotions. In fact, our feelings are often major targets we shame. That's the focus of the next chapter.

9
Released from Shaming Our Feelings

I *feel so ripped off,"* Keith *murmured in a soft, flat voice.* "*I saw a medical* show the other night. A doctor inserted a long needle directly into a guy's heart to stimulate it. I thought, 'Yeah, that's what happened to me.' The big difference is that my heart injection wasn't meant to stimulate. It was as though Novocain had been injected into my heart and all my feelings went numb. Not just the bad ones; the good ones too. And I feel ripped off."

Keith was raised by impaired parents who created an emotionally starved environment for him. He is beginning to realize the effects of his emotional anemia: inability to feel emotions beyond a vague "good" or "bad." In a sense, Keith *has* been ripped off because the capacity to experience a wide range of authentic emotions is part of our God-given human heritage.

The Biblical Model

"A time to weep and a time to laugh, a time to mourn and a time to dance" (Ecclesiastes 3:4) is the scriptural portrait of great joy and deep grief in the broad panorama of human emotional experiences. And heroes of the faith in both the Old Testament and New Testament displayed a wide range of heartfelt emotions. Just think of David dancing with joy before the Ark of the Covenant (2 Samuel 6:12-14) and wailing in despair over Absalom's death (2 Samuel 18:33—19:1).

Jesus, the supreme example of a perfectly balanced human being, rejoiced and grieved and got furious. In each situation, Jesus responded appropriately and authentically to his emotions.[1] Therefore, we can say confidently that God expects us to appropriately express the full range of human emotions.

So why are you and I often so uncomfortable with feelings? Because when it comes to feeling and expressing emotions, it appears that even we *Christian* adult children are guided more by our earthly parents than our heavenly parent. As children in dysfunctional families, we learned to see ourselves as disobedient and disloyal if we expressed any emotions lacking the parental seal of approval.

When Feelings Seem Disobedient, Disloyal and Dangerous

If we grew up in families where feelings were a luxury we couldn't afford, we still may be living emotionally impoverished lives in an attempt to be loyal. If our parents and siblings keep up the myth of the happy family, we might be seen as traitors for discovering feelings that suggest an alternative interpretation of our growing-up years.

But even beyond the discomfort of experiencing ourselves as disobedient and disloyal, we might experience feeling strong emotions as *dangerous*. In extremely dysfunctional families, children learn that strong feelings usually directly and immediately cause harmful behavior. If our only adult models express emotions violently, we will think the only outcome of *experiencing* a strong feeling is destructively *expressing* that feeling. You might even be getting anxious just *reading* about feeling strong emotions.

Thinking that feelings are dangerous is particularly applicable to three areas of life: fear, grief and anger. Most of us adult children learned to shame ourselves for experiencing these major emotions. In the following pages we'll see how that works out in our adult lives.

When We Shame Our Fears

Fear became the core emotion of all human beings when sin entered the world. The first human emotion after the Fall is described in Genesis 3:10 where we hear Adam say, "I was afraid."

I am not saying all fear is sinful or harmful. Healthy fear prevents us from walking in front of speeding cars or leaning on hot stoves. And fear, that is to say reverential awe of God, protects us from making some clearly wrong, sinful choices.

Fear comes in a variety of kinds and degrees. We might fear embarrassment, rejection, failure, even success. We might fear fear itself. Sometimes fear wears a recognizable face, such as fear of snakes or heights. Often this face is a facade covering a deeper, destructive fear of abandonment.

Fear of Abandonment

If we look for the foundational fear underlying all the others that cower and cripple us, I think we usually find fear of abandonment. To trace one of our destructive fears to its roots, we must ask: Why is that so frightening? Most of us never even see how fear of abandonment runs our lives.

For instance, does the following progression of thoughts remind you of yourself?

Imagine that you have just been asked by a dear friend to do something for which you have neither the time nor the inclination. You want to say no, but you are afraid. Why is saying no so bad?

You might experience his or her disapproval. Why is that so bad?

He or she might not like you anymore. Why is that so bad?

He or she would not want to be your friend and spend time with you anymore. Why is that so bad?

You would be alone.

Now, we're getting close. Loneliness is one of the "trigger events" for fear of abandonment. Trigger events are situations which symbolize or resemble an earlier trauma which was perceived as life-threatening.

In well-functioning homes, parents consistently provide adequate emotional and physical nurturing to protect children from experiencing traumatizing abandonment. However, if children experience abandonment with enough frequency and intensity in childhood, it becomes a significant trauma which will mark the adult child's life with a strong fear of re-experiencing *any* reminder of abandonment.[2]

Survivors of concentration camps and combat often experience post-traumatic stress; it's reasonable to assume that child-abuse survivors do also. And the more intense the abuse we survived, the more intense our fear of abandonment. But in addition to the physical and emotional potential for fear of abandonment, we might also be *spiritually* pre-disposed to it.

Sin and Fear of Abandonment

When Adam and Eve sinned, their separation from God also brought fear of abandonment by God. When we study the Scriptures, we see that God is very concerned about the destructive impact of fear in our lives. There are several hundred "fear nots" in the Bible, and many of them specifically speak to fear of abandonment and its spiritual antecedent, separation from God. For example, Isaiah 41:10 tells us, "Do not fear, for I am with you; do not be dismayed, for I am your God."

And, within the context of God's concern for our fear of abandonment, it is particularly significant that Jesus was called "Immanuel," which means God *with* us. (See Matthew 1:23.)

Clearly, faith in Jesus is the solution to the spiritual roots of fear of abandonment. Jesus was careful to address this fear in his disciples as he prepared to die. Knowing his imminent death would trigger their fear of abandonment, Jesus proved that he understood the depth of their need for him; he assured them he would not orphan them. Rather than leave them alone, he would give them the constant companionship of his Holy Spirit (see John 14).

Feeling like Orphans

Many adult children feel like emotional orphans when they experience fear of abandonment. You might have noticed this in your own life. I know I have.

A few years ago during a particularly stressful time in my life, my husband and I got separated while we were shopping in a large mall. Ordinarily, this wouldn't have bothered me. But that day I became overwhelmed with my frightening, orphaned-child feelings. I went from shop to shop searching for Garth, feeling more panicky with each passing minute. I was sobbing by the time I finally found him. The intensity of my feelings of abandonment surprised and embarrassed me.

Another woman, Charlotte, was able to tie her adult experience to its specific trigger events.

"I know it's dumb, but when my friend forgot our lunch date, I felt like a scared, lonely little kid. I sat in the restaurant and waited and waited while my heart was pounding. I wanted to cry. It makes me feel so stupid to admit this, because I am not a little kid. I am a grown woman."

When I asked Charlotte how old she felt while waiting in the restaurant, she replied without hesitation. "I felt five years old. That's when everything fell apart at home. My folks got divorced, and my mother had a nervous breakdown."

Do you shame yourself when you become painfully aware that you feel like a frightened, abandoned child? If so, you might fear unpleasant feelings in general and "losing control" in particular.

Fear of Feelings and Needs

Adult children are usually described as compulsive controllers. They often try to supervise and regulate every detail of their own and others' behaviors. Since they went through childhood with little or no control, it is as if they have silently vowed, "Never again." If this is your style, you are what has been called an "external controller."

However, even if you do not *appear* to be controlling, you might be an "internal controller," dedicated to extinguishing any awareness of your personal needs by withholding your feelings. As we have seen, impaired parents are so absorbed with their own needs that they don't have any emotional energy to meet their children's needs. It is too painful and scary for these children to consistently have their legitimate needs unmet, so they try to be need-free. Shaming their human needs might seem to work for years. But they will always be in danger of experiencing something that penetrates their need-free defenses. That's what happened to Sarah.

As a child, Sarah was emotionally abandoned by both parents, and she learned to disown her legitimate needs for companionship, encouragement and comfort. As an adult, Sarah is beginning to acknowledge that those are appropriate human needs, even though her fear of feelings and needs continues to be a powerful force.

"It was disgusting and stupid. Why was she crying, and why did she obviously enjoy putting her head on her husband's shoulder and having his arms around her? I can't imagine ever wanting anyone to do that for me." Sarah was describing her response to seeing a husband comfort his distressed wife.

"See, this is what I've figured out," Sarah told me. "If I need that stuff now, that means I needed it back then and didn't get it. I can't stand the pain that brings. It's just a whole lot easier to not have any needs or feelings."

How can you argue with logic like that?

The problem is that fearing and denying our natural human needs and feelings prevents us from being fully the way God created us. So how can we be more *real*, more fully human? We begin to own and experience those painful, unmet needs and the emotions that accompany them. Often, one of these emotions is sadness.

Shaming Our Sadness

You do not have to be raised in an extremely dysfunctional home to be an expert at shaming your own sadness and other unpleasant emotions. Carly does a superb job, and she was raised by loving parents.

Carly's parents were sincere Christians and deeply committed denominational leaders. At an early age, Carly learned to love Jesus, serve others and disown her unpleasant feelings. She described one vivid memory that "summarized" her childhood.

"My folks and I had been at a church conference and summer camp thing for nearly a week. I was pretty little—not in school yet. It was hot, and I hadn't been with my folks much all week. Just with baby sitters who were fine, but complete strangers. By Friday, I was really tired, lonely and generally upset, I guess. Anyway, I remember that I started to cry and cause a scene, and my folks looked very embarrassed. My mom bent down and reminded me that it was Friday and Friday was 'Smile Day.'

"What you need to know is that *every* day of the week was 'Smile Day' when I was growing up. So whenever mom asked, 'What day is it?' I was supposed to answer cheerily, 'It's Smile Day.' As I look back, I remember feeling truly guilty if I was not always smiling—I mean *always* smiling. And the funny thing is, I still do."

It has been difficult for Carly to give up shaming her sadness and learn that a Christian concept of joy is not synonymous with wearing a perpetual plastic smile.

George wasn't given the "every day is Smile Day" treatment, but he became an accomplished sadness shamer for reasons of his own.

"I can't believe how I reacted. It's a good thing no one else was around, or I'd have felt like an even bigger fool." George was telling the support group about his reactions to seeing a father and son fishing together. "I couldn't take my eyes off them. The father was so patient and gentle with the kid. My face started to feel hot, and I broke down." George's voice cracked, and he turned away to conceal his tears. "I'm really sorry for breaking down again like this."

What George termed "breaking down," I call appropriate grieving. George was raised with an alcoholic father who never had time to take him fishing or anywhere else. Although he had experienced a profound sense of father loss as a child, George had not yet given himself permission to grieve.

Old Patterns, Old Pain

Like Carly and George, you might have grown up in a family that only allowed pleasant emotions. No matter how much certain Christians spiritualize being happy all the time, Romans 12:15 calls us to "rejoice with those who rejoice; mourn with those who mourn." But Carly's and George's families rewrote this verse to read "Rejoice with those who rejoice." Period.

How can you tell if you are shaming your sadness? If you let yourself cry only when you are alone and then refer to your crying as "breaking down," you are probably a card-carrying self-shamer.

Barb never cried around other people because it hurt too much to have to ask for some comfort and then not get it. She sat alone in her closet when she wanted to cry. Now an adult, she's set up the same pattern in her marriage by only crying when her husband and she are having a fight—a time when he's too angry to offer comfort. He even says, "Go into the other room if you're going to cry," just as her parents used to say.

One evening, Barb was reading a book that stirred up childhood memories, but she didn't cry until after her husband had gone to sleep. Then she came downstairs and "broke down," once again crying alone with no one to comfort her.

I invited Barb to consider reading her book, letting the tears of repressed childhood grief come and asking her husband to hold and comfort her without saying anything to try to take away her sadness. Although that idea was terrifying at first, Barb tried it. She was surprised how much easier it was for her husband to offer comfort when he found out that he did not have to be responsible for eliminating her painful feelings.

Like Barb, many adult children have deep pools of sadness resulting from childhood losses they've never mourned. I am convinced that some of us trudge through our adult lives chronically depressed because we have not done the intensely painful grief work we need to do. This might be especially true for those of us who need to grieve the loss of our fathers.

My own depression lessened significantly after I began to consciously acknowledge and grieve losing the father I never knew. But I certainly have not fully drained my pool of pain from losing my father. Recently, when I heard a song about a loving relationship between a father and daughter, I had to pull off the highway because I was crying too hard to see. That was an intensely painful experience, but I felt a genuine sense of release when I allowed myself to mourn. If your early years included parental abuse and consistent emotional abandonment, you experienced a betrayal of trust that deeply lacerated your life. When parents betray and reject you, soul-stabbing grief might threaten to overwhelm. As a child, you had to repress that sorrow to survive. As an adult, you might still stifle and shame this sadness to protect yourself from emotional pain and to project an image of being strong, in control and mature.

Confusion Is Common
Feelings cannot be separated into tidy bundles like dark and light clothes on wash day. They tumble together, leaving us feeling "crazy and mixed-up," as Jolene, an incest survivor, described it to our therapy group.

"I feel like I am going out of my mind. My feelings are all crazy and mixed-up. I just found out from my aunt that my mother was molested by a neighbor man. Her folks never told the police or let on that it happened. And all her mother, my grandma, said to her was, 'Stay away from there.' Nobody paid any attention to my mom's feelings." Jolene was crying too hard to continue.

After a few moments, she said, "I am so confused about what I feel toward my mom now. I am furiously angry at her for not protecting me from my uncle's molesting me over and over. But I feel pity for her too. I especially feel bad because I am getting some help and she has carried her hurt inside all these years."

For Jolene, sadness and anger shared the emotional limelight. For other adult children, anger either takes center stage or is banished to the wings.

Shaming Our Anger

"Let's talk about anger," I said to the group.

"I'm angry all the time at everyone," proclaimed the son of excessively rigid and perfectionistic parents.

"I don't think I've ever been angry," an incest survivor said softly.

Have you noticed that anger seems to be the only emotion some adult children ever feel, while for others it is the one "dangerous" emotion they never allow themselves to experience?

When Anger Is Appropriate

Anger is not a sin. Did you know that? More important, do you believe that?

We've already seen that Jesus felt anger and acted appropriately on his feelings. And hundreds of times in the Scriptures, God is described as experiencing and expressing anger. For example, God responds with anger at injustice and victimization, at disobedience to him and at idolatry,[3] among other sinful attitudes and acts.

When we witness the effects of injustice, disobedience to God and/ or idolatry, I believe that anger is an appropriate response. For example, do you think you would feel angry if you had to watch helplessly as someone beat or raped a child? Of course you would, because that is such blatant injustice and victimization. Or what if you observed a father consistently abuse his children emotionally and verbally in such a way that the children became very discouraged and you knew the father's behavior was directly disobedient to scriptural principles? I suspect that situation would anger you too. How about if you saw parents teaching their children to worship false gods? I think that would anger you as well because idolatry is wrong and because you know that the parents are causing their children to "stumble" with devastating consequences.

Let's take this one step closer to home. I believe that anger is appropriate, not only when we *witness* the effects of injustice and victimization, disobedience to God and idolatry, but when we *experience* those effects ourselves. Why in the world isn't it appropriate for you to feel anger toward the perpetrator(s) if you were physically and/or sexually abused as a child? In effect, you had to stand by helplessly and watch a child be victimized. *That child was you.* Does it make those heinous acts of victimization any less unjust because they happened to *you* instead of to another child?

Time Out

God is angry about the abuse you endured as a child. I invite you to consider re-examining the scene of your abuse from God's perspective. *God knows it was not your fault, no matter what your abuser told you!* If you have never tried to look at your abuse this way, you might want to find a trusted friend, a pastor or a counselor who could provide support and comfort as you experience the anger, sadness and other feelings that might emerge.

Please remember, you will not feel these emotions with such overwhelming intensity *forever.* Giving yourself permission to cry, shout, talk and write them out seems to help.

Even if you were not physically or sexually abused, it is appropriate to feel anger if your parents caused you to stumble into sinful patterns of thinking and behaving. The difficult thing is to handle your anger appropriately.

God's anger is always appropriate and justified, and he never responds to it with sin. Unfortunately, the same cannot be said about our anger. As we have seen, God does not equate our anger with sin, but he does issue a warning because anger is such a powerful emotion: "In your anger do not sin . . ." (Ephesians 4:26). Anger ceases being appropriate and becomes sinful when it becomes a habitual attitude rather than the appropriate emotional response to injustice and the other situations examined earlier.

When anger habitually dominates our lives, it is serving an unseen, defensive purpose. Anger can be used to shield us against anticipated pain in a defensive response to previous pain. This habitual, defensive anger can hurt us and those closest to us.

Marcie was raised by a controlling, workaholic father and a sweetly manipulative mother. Anger was the armor Marcie wore into conflict as she battled to win respect from her parents.

Finally, Marcie realized why she didn't want to give up her anger toward her parents. It made her feel safe and strong because she felt unable to set limits or say no unless she was angry. When she would get angry and tell her parents off, they would back down for awhile. Later Marcie could apologize for what she had said and blame her comments on the anger, as if she didn't really have those thoughts. ("It was all the anger's fault.") Marcie believed that letting go of her anger would be dropping her shield. She would have to admit she hated the way her parents try to run her life.

Perhaps you use anger to shield yourself from taking personal responsibility for your desire to set healthy, appropriate boundaries with important and intrusive people in your life. This self-protective use of anger might be an attempt to avoid that important person's disapproval or rejection. Those responses can trigger our painful feelings of abandonment.

You might also use anger to pump up your self-image when you feel small or scared or stupid. Lots of us do. Remember the insecure little man who turned out to be the Wizard of Oz? He stood behind a curtain, pulling and twisting a lot of handles and dials while a ferocious, powerful-looking image out front huffed and puffed, causing everyone to cower from a distance. Perhaps the real you, feeling small and weak, stands behind the curtain of your anger while the huffing and puffing mask looks big and tough.

If you were shamed as a child for being a "cry baby," you might impersonate the Wizard of Oz with your anger whenever you begin to be aware of feeling authentic sadness. And the more shame-bound you are, the more likely you are to respond with anger in situations that you interpret as critical commentaries on your inadequacy, incompetence or general worthlessness.

Psychologist Richard Lazarus suggests that this kind of habitual anger and hostile lifestyle magnifies certain kinds of daily hassles and might be a health hazard. Lazarus asserts that researchers in the past were too shortsighted when they determined stress levels by simply adding up points assigned to various life events.

[Lazarus said:] "What's stressful to one person may be no more than a minor inconvenience to another." . . . Lazarus found that *hassles that tap personal weaknesses* often cause more stress and may be more health-endangering.[4]

Lazarus, and others, have concluded that daily hassles bother people more when they feel helpless. And habitual anger is a common approach to habitual feelings of helplessness. For adult children, feelings of helplessness might be trigger events that stir our memories of childhood trauma. The feelings of helplessness are too frightening and painful, so we use anger as a defensive smoke screen. This might appear to protect us from painful emotions, but habitual anger exacts a toll in damaged relationships and stress-related illnesses. Certainly, not all adult children use anger to defend against the pain of other disowned emotions; many of us have also disowned our anger too. Instead, we might use various addictions to numb all our feelings.

Medicating with Addictions

Earlier we saw that people tend to use masks of perfection in a shame-based attempt to hide the flaws they despise. It's also common for people to use medicating addictions to attempt to handle feelings they would like to disown.

All addictions, legal or illegal, are attempts to self-medicate the pain of living. The more unrecognized shame and unresolved pain we have in our lives, the greater our needs for the emotional anesthesia that addictions provide.

One expert in psychopharmacology asserts that all human and non-human species possess a drive to alter mood and consciousness. This drive is as powerful as the drives of sex, thirst and hunger. His research revealed that during the Vietnam War the water buffalo nibbled opium poppies more often than they normally do.[5]

Romans 8:22 describes the "whole creation . . . groaning as in the pains of childbirth right up to the present time." It appears that even the water buffalo were self-medicating the pain of living in a war zone. They used a substance that was effective, predictable and available. Those are qualities we always seek in any addictive substance or compulsive behavior.

For ease of discussion, I will divide addictions into internal and external categories. And while there are differences, there are more similarities between the two.

Internal Addictions
Internal addictions includes all the legal and illegal substances we traditionally have considered addictive, such as alcohol and other drugs, nicotine, caffeine and even prescription tranquilizers. All these substances alter our moods through biochemical manipulation of chemical messengers in our brains.

Recent research suggests that even ice cream and other culturally acceptable substances work on the same brain receptors responsible for drug addiction. According to Dr. Adam Drewnowsky, you can blame sugar and fat which combine to "create a compulsion less intense than drug addiction but which works on the same principle. Both, he says, trigger the brain's pleasure mechanisms, thereby giving a sort of good all over feeling. . . ."[6]

Some of us have known for a long time that our occasional (or constant) overeating is an attempt to satisfy an emotional need rather than to satisfy our physical appetites. In my own case, for nearly three months after my mother was diagnosed with cancer last year, I anesthetized my emotional pain with Hershey bars. Instead of relying on God's comfort, I was, in effect, practicing medicine without a license by prescribing and administering chocolate tranquilizers.

In addition to these internal addictions, there are external, behavioral addictions, many of which also seem to produce biochemical changes in our brains.[7]

External Addictions

In his thought-provoking book, *The Addictive Personality*, Craig Nakken asks and answers a critical question:

What do different objects and events (eating, gambling, chemicals and sex) that people can get addicted to have in common? It's their ability to produce a positive and pleasurable mood change. This is where one finds the addictive potential of an object or event.[8]

With this in mind, we are probably not surprised to learn that adult children from dysfunctional families, often desperate for a "positive and pleasurable mood change," use a diverse array of external addictions. Some are denounced sincerely from church pulpits by clergy who self-medicate their *own* unfaced emotions with more accepted external addictions.

For example, sexual promiscuity is rightly condemned as a degrading, dehumanizing and destructive perversion of one of God's best gifts. But staying in an abusive relationship might be applauded as "Christian compassion." Similarly, gambling is declared "off limits" for Christians, while the devastating effects of compulsive shopping and overspending are virtually ignored. Recently, even workaholism has come in for some appropriate censure in Christian circles. However, few church spokespersons have had the courage to highlight the compulsive and addictive qualities of the sanctified workaholism and ecclesiastical hyperactivity that often masquerade as deep religious commitment.

I have pictured a dark cycle of emotional pain and anesthetizing addictions that produce their own pain. The truth is that in a fallen world *life brings pain*. Remember, you and I and even the water buffalo are all groaning as a result of sin. This is what could be called appropriate and unavoidable pain given the situations we face.

Life Brings Appropriate, Unavoidable Pain

Using chemicals to manipulate our moods to avoid feeling any emotional pain is a futile attempt to deny how sin has devastated this planet. Instead of chemically camouflaging our pain, we need to acknowledge it and allow it to draw us to God, "the Father of compassion and the God of all comfort." (See 2 Corinthians 1:3-4.)

It's a sad fact that people from dysfunctional families usually enter their adult lives with even *deeper* pools of childhood pain than are the normal "occupational hazards" of being human. Though the subtle or severe abuse these children endured in childhood was inappropriate and avoidable, the painful emotions stirred up are valid and cannot be avoided. For instance, deep sadness is an appropriate and unavoidable emotional response to a parent's betrayal of trust.

If you are an adult child from one of these pain-filled families, perhaps you've dealt with your deep pool of old pain by attempting to deny and deaden it with substances and/or activities. The irony of this solution is that attempts to escape from *appropriate* and *unavoidable* pain always produce *inappropriate* and *avoidable* pain. Since denying and deadening appropriate pain never resolves it, the net result is that you simply compound your pain by adding new layers of pain. For example, if you continually use alcohol to deaden the old pain of ungrieved childhood losses, you will soon add the inappropriate, avoidable pain of chemical dependency to your pool of pain.

Change begins with new choices to "drain" that pool of appropriate, unavoidable pain so that we have less need for anesthetizing addictions which bring pain of their own.

New Choices for Change
In recent years, many psychologists have emphasized the strategic role of thought patterns in determining emotions and choices. This is old news to Bible students familiar with passages that teach the same truth.[9]

As recovering adult children from dysfunctional families, we must begin to think and live the truth about our feelings. When we do, we will experience more authentic emotions and make healthier behavioral choices.

Here are a few examples of old, shame-bound lies and new, shame-free truths.

Shame-bound Lies	*Shame-free Truths*
Emotions are unnecessary, bothersome and embarrassing.	Emotions are a gift from God and an integral part of my human nature which reflects his image.
Emotions are bad and dangerous, so I am safer when I avoid them.	Emotions are neither good nor bad. Emotions can be expressed appropriately, and I can learn to do that. I am less of what God created me to be when I avoid feeling emotions.
If I begin to feel my emotions, I will go crazy.	When I am able to feel my emotions, I will become more authentic and alive.
It is stupid to get all upset over things that happened years ago. It is best to "let sleeping dogs lie."	It is appropriate for children to feel confused, afraid, sad and/or angry when their parents neglect and/or abuse them. Those feelings did not go away just because I had to learn to deaden and disown them. They are still inside, and they are affecting my life today. It is best to face and feel them honestly.
When I felt sad as a child, no one was there for me. I couldn't stand to feel that despair and loneliness again.	I have resources now as an adult that I did not have as a child. I can find more reliable (although not perfect) human comforters. And I know (or can know) God personally and have his comfort. It will be painful to grieve childhood losses, but I can stand it.
I was told as a child I should never be angry, and I know God is angry about my anger—both my anger about the past and current situations.	It is appropriate to feel angry about what angers God. Misleading and/or abusing children angers God. I can learn to express anger appropriately and without sinning.
Unless I explode with anger, people will walk all over me.	I can learn appropriate, boundary-setting techniques so that I don't have to hide behind my shield of anger.

Begin listing *your* current ideas about emotions. Then examine those beliefs for telltale signs of shame and denial of truth. You might need to ask someone you think is more objective and less shame-bound than you to help you evaluate your ideas about emotions. Identifying and changing our shame-based misbeliefs about emotions will begin to release us from shaming our feelings. But there is more we can do to drain that pool of pain.

What we believe about emotions affects how we act in handling our emotions. The more shame-free and truthful these beliefs and decisions are, the healthier our behaviors will be.

New Choices to Express Feelings

The following suggestions are only a few examples of new behaviors that might help you experience and express your authentic human emotions more comfortably. Use them to "prime the pump" as you continue to drain your pool of personal pain.

1. Prepare an inventory of the addictions which you use to deaden your emotions. See pages 118-19 for examples of internal and external addictions. If you are serious about changing your patterns of shaming authentic emotions, you must begin to practice more addiction-free living.

The most harmful addictions are also the most effective emotional anesthetics. You cannot get very far in recovering from shame and other effects of growing up in a dysfunctional family if you continue to use these heavy-duty addictions, such as alcohol, cocaine, etc.

2. Get help immediately to stop using the deadly addictions listed above. Do not try to do it alone. Getting support is a critical component of the change process.

3. Also, get help for your addiction if *food* is your drug of choice. This addiction can be deadly too. If you have been "stuffing your feelings" by stuffing your face, you will need more than a calorie counter to change. Find a program designed to alter your nutritional habits and help you find healthier ways to handle your feelings. Food will never satisfy emotional and spiritual hunger.

4. Get a photograph of yourself before the age of ten. Study it, and notice how small you were. (If you are working with a counselor, you might want to do this during a session.) Allow yourself to remember

how confused, scared, sad and lonely (maybe even angry) you sometimes felt. Ask the child in the picture what was needed years ago when feeling those distressing emotions. If possible, make arrangements to secure those things now to provide emotional support and comfort in your current life. For example, buy a teddy bear and/or a pet to cuddle and talk to anytime you are feeling these emotions. Find a trusted friend or counselor you can arrange to see or phone (at mutually acceptable times) to pour out your heart. Find a trustworthy person who can give "safe hugs" when you want them.

5. Write a statement of truth about your fear of abandonment. This should reflect the changed realities of your current adult life. Keep a copy of this with you at all times to read to that frightened child inside of you that reacts so intensely to events that trigger feelings of abandonment. (Do not shame these feelings of abandonment; that's what you probably *have* been doing. Remember, you are practicing new, *shame-free* choices about how to handle your feelings.) Here is a sample of such a statement.

The Truth about Abandonment

I am feeling upset and scared right now because something happened that reminded me of how alone and terrified I sometimes felt as a child. I don't like this feeling, but I know that I will survive experiencing it, and it will pass.

The truth is: Now, *as an adult,* I cannot be abandoned in the same way I could have been as a child. I am safe. What a relief!

The truth is: I might be jilted, stood up, dumped, slighted, forgotten about, ignored, left behind and even cruelly rejected, but I can survive all of these painful experiences.

The truth is: God will never leave, forsake nor abandon me.

Figure 9-1.

6. If you currently handle your anger by exploding, practice something different and less harmful to you and those closest to you. First, try exercising. Vigorous exercise releases the energy that anger usually produces. You can bike, jog, wash your car or even wash windows.

Then write about your angry feelings. Practice identifying the under-lying cause(s), such as experiencing injustice, feeling helpless, etc. If you find writing difficult, you might want to draw or finger paint pictures about your angry feelings. Black and red crayons, markers or paints are especially suitable for this.

7. Learn some respectful assertiveness techniques so you don't need anger to shield you from personal boundary violations. Try the "broken record" (you continue to matter-of-factly state your desire or prefer-ence until the boundary-invading "other" realizes you are not backing-down).

The following example of the broken record is similar to those some of my clients have used successfully—but *not* painlessly. Though only one side of the conversation is given here, you'll get the full gist.

"Yes, Mother, I know you assumed I would be spending Thanks-giving Day with you and Dad as I have for twenty-eight years. That's why I'm telling you that I am going skiing with friends this year. . . .

"I can tell you are shocked and disappointed that I am going skiing with friends at Thanksgiving this year. I will be leaving on Tuesday afternoon. . . .

"My spending Thanksgiving with friends does *not* mean I have out-grown my family. It means I am going to go skiing this year. . . .

"I can imagine that I do sound like a broken record, and no, I will not be changing my mind. I am going skiing this year. . . .

"I hope you decide to change your mind about staying in your room all day and choose to enjoy the day instead. But, of course, you are an adult and entitled to make your own choices. I need to leave now."

8. Increase your feeling vocabulary by preparing a list of pleasant and unpleasant emotions. This will help you talk and write about the wider range of emotions you will be experiencing. Because we adult children tend to be so all-or-nothing about everything, including emotions, it is necessary to learn to identify feelings of differing intensities. Figure 9-2 is a small sample of such a vocabulary list.

Sample Feeling Vocabulary List[10]

Pleasant Feelings			Unpleasant Feelings		
Strong	Moderate	Mild	Mild	Moderate	Strong
Loved	Liked	Regarded	Unpopular	Disliked	Loathed
Love	Affection	Friendliness	Unfriendliness	Aversion	Hatred
Euphoria	Happiness	Contentment	Discontentment	Sadness	Despair
Vibrancy	Excitement	Alertness	Lethargy	Dejection	Misery

Figure 9-2.

These examples will probably suggest many other behaviors you can practice to begin eliminating ways you shame your feelings. Celebrate your capacity to feel a full range of emotions. God created you to do so, and he will sustain and strengthen you as you work toward that goal.

Personal Reflection

Think through the following questions:

☐ What messages about feelings did I get in my family as a child?

☐ What messages about feelings do I give myself currently?

☐ What do I use to defend myself against "dangerous" feelings?

☐ Will I begin practicing one of the change choices listed above? If so, which one? When?

After reading and thinking about emotions, some of your "frozen feelings" might be starting to thaw. You might be feeling a lot of confusing, conflicting emotions for the first time in your adult life. You might even think this means that you are going crazy. *In reality, it means that you are feeling a lot of confusing, conflicting emotions for the first time in your adult life.*

Having these confusing, conflicting, new feelings does not mean you are going crazy or losing control. It means you are becoming more fully the person God created you to be.

☐ Thank God for creating you with an emotional nature, and ask him to guide and comfort you as you begin to understand and accept it.

Looking Ahead

When you begin practicing new, shame-free attitudes and actions concerning your personal flaws and feelings, you will develop a more respectful, healthy and biblical perspective toward yourself. You will diminish your need to "play to the crowd" by using others to applaud the way you perform and please.

As you are increasingly released from self-shaming, you will be able to form increasingly shame-free relationships. Now *there's* a goal worth pursuing. The next chapter will help you do just that.

10
Released
from Shame-based
Codependency

*C*raig is the brilliant son of an alcoholic father. His fiancé, Lorraine, is bulimic. As a fourth-year medical student, Craig understands the damage Lorraine's body sustains with each binging and purging cycle. And Craig is determined to make her stop. Craig has lost contact with his friends, and his studies are suffering because he spends so much time monitoring Lorraine's eating disorder. Craig is convinced that he can change Lorraine if he loves her enough and tries hard enough.

"How can I feel good about myself, be happy or think about helping others if I can't even help the girl I love?" Craig asked.

Craig is sincere. Craig is deeply motivated. Craig is also codependent.

Codependency is a shame-based, painful pattern of dependence on others to provide a sense of personal safety, identity and worth. Codependency binds us to relationships where we are being disrespected and controlled by people we, in turn, disrespect and attempt to control. It is "other addiction."

Other Addiction

How can you tell if you are one of the millions of codependent "other addicts" who tend to get compulsively overinvolved with others? There's a story of one woman who discovered she was in a codependent relationship with her boyfriend when she had a near-death experience and *his* life flashed before her eyes!

Use the following quiz to assess *your* own level of codependent "other addiction."

Other Addiction Quiz

Check the statements that are true of you:

_____ 1. My good feelings about myself depend on having the approval of others.

_____ 2. I believe my main purpose in life is to solve the problems and relieve the pain of others.

_____ 3. I value the opinions and preferences of others more than my own.

_____ 4. I feel uneasy and "empty" if I am not in a close relationship.

_____ 5. I sacrifice my values and standards in order to stay connected with others.

_____ 6. My fear of anger, criticism and rejection dictates what I do and say.

_____ 7. My interests are usually put aside so I can pursue the interests of others.

_____ 8. I believe I am being selfish when I want to do something just for myself.

_____ 9. I give money and gifts as a way to feel more secure in relationships.

_____ 10. I spend a lot of mental energy trying to get others to do things my way without having them know or get angry (for their own good).

———— **11.** I try to anticipate others' needs and desires and meet those needs and desires before the other people have to ask.

———— **12.** My mood and sense of well-being are directly related to those of others; I can't feel good if someone else feels bad.

———— **13.** I spend so much time helping others that my job, family, health, etc., suffer.

———— **14.** I spend little time or energy considering my emotional state and a great deal considering that of others.

———— **15.** I often have to explain or excuse the person closest to me to myself or friends.

———— **16.** My needs never seem as important and urgent as the needs of others.

———— **17.** I have changed my hairstyle and/or way of dressing to please others.

———— **18.** I believe many of the people in my life would be lost without me since I protect them from the effects of their stupid, silly and/or sinful choices.

———— **19.** I have remained in one or more adult relationships without seeking help to change it after being slapped, punched, kicked or otherwise physically abused.

———— **20.** My most significant relationships seem to have a pattern; for instance, they begin and/or end the same way, leaving me with the same bad feelings about myself.

SCORING: One to six *suggests mild, manageable codependency.* Seven to thirteen *indicates moderate and increasingly unmanageable codependency.* Fourteen to nineteen *strongly suggests that your other addiction has become unmanageable and you need help to change your codependent relational style.*
If you have a score of twenty, *please seek help immediately.*

If you are upset about your score on the Other Addiction Quiz, don't despair. *You were not born with codependency chromosomes. You learned codependent relational patterns as a child.* You live what you learn, and now as an adult you can learn healthier, more respectful and biblical relational patterns. But it won't be easy, because other addiction is more powerful and subtly seductive than other kinds of addictions. Even if you can "just say no" to drugs, you might have a difficult time just saying no to people—and for good reason.

Codependency and Relational Needs

We were created to be in relationships with other relational beings, not with chemical substances. We have relational natures because we are created in the image of God, who is relational. We see this in the Triune Godhead—Father, Son and Holy Spirit.

Ideally, our relational natures draw us to God and compel us to fulfill appropriate responsibilities to others. But sin always shatters the ideal. When sin entered the world, God's image was not withdrawn from human beings, but it was broken almost beyond recognition. This truth is seen dramatically in some of the self-destructive patterns that express our sin-shattered relational natures. These wretched relational patterns are handed down from generation to generation. And today we called these patterns *codependency*.

I am *not* saying that all relationships are codependent. Consistently adequate parents teach their children appropriate and respectful patterns of relating to themselves and others. Obviously, neither the parents, the children nor their relationships will be perfect and completely free from the effects of sin. But they will not be in bondage to shame and codependency.

Binding Shame and the Codependency Connection

I defined codependency as a shame-based, painful pattern of dependence on others to provide a sense of personal safety, identity and worth. As you reflect on the effects of binding shame, can you see how it paves the way for codependency?

Feeding on our God-given relational needs, the binding shame we learned in our dysfunctional families causes existence guilt ("I don't deserve to be with others") and fear of abandonment ("I'll die if I'm not with others"). Instead of developing healthy relationships, we develop the same kinds of relationships that were modeled for us—ones based on shame and codependence.

When codependency flourishes in our lives, we appear to relate to others based on this progression of beliefs:

1. "I don't deserve to be connected to you because I am a worthless

non-person."

2. "I feel as if I'll die if I'm not connected to you because you make me feel safe from abandonment and give me a sense of identity and worth."

3. "So I'll do anything and everything to maintain the connection to you."

Having learned as children to survive by maintaining this self-protective focus on others, this pattern becomes the template shaping all our adult interactions. Many adult children have noticed that, to some degree, all our current relationships resemble family reunions. Only the names and faces change.

Just as there are degrees of family dysfunction and binding shame, there are degrees of codependency in adult children. This continuum of codependent functioning ranges from those adults who are basically healthy but exhibit occasional codependent behaviors to those who are consistently and compulsively codependent. Our places on the codependency continuum correspond to the degrees of distorted thinking we inherited from our families. For as someone has observed, codependency is a *relative* thing!

As adult children from dysfunctional families, we are caught in an undercurrent of shame-bound thinking that carries us down a rushing river of disrespectful relationships. This chapter is about how to stop "going with the flow" of learned codependency and how to start swimming upstream against childhood lessons by forming mutually respectful relationships. Let's start by examining healthy relationships.

Healthy Relationships

When people exhibit realistic respect for themselves and for others, they have the basis for healthy relationships. In mutually respectful relationships, we uphold the other's right to separate choices and opinions, so neither attempts to control or manipulate. We can do this because we respect our own choices and opinions and don't need to have them constantly validated by blatantly or subtly forcing others to agree with us.

Respecting ourselves and others also requires that we allow other adults to be as responsible for the consequences of their choices as we are for ours.

Time Out

Stop and ask yourself if you are trying to rescue some adult—a relative or friend— from experiencing the consequences of his or her irresponsible choices.

You might care deeply about this person and believe you are expressing true Christian compassion. Can you see that you are actually expressing disrespect? When you rescue someone, you are saying, "I believe you are less capable of living responsibly than I am. You are like a child or a mentally retarded adult." Is this what you really believe?

Ask God to help you recognize and relinquish your rescuing.

Let me highlight an important point. Respecting others does *not* mean we must admire or tolerate everything others do. It is extremely important to balance the emphasis on mutual respect with realistic understanding of human nature. We respect others because they bear God's image and are the objects of his love. However, that image is marred by a sin nature. And others might reject God's love.

The healthiest interpersonal relationships are based on *realistic* respect for ourselves and for others. God says that human hearts are "deceitful above all things" (Jeremiah 17:9) and this means that *any* person's sinful, deceitful heart is capable of enormous evil. It is not realistic to expect every person we meet to be kind, honest and trustworthy. This attitude is neither appropriate trust nor realistic respect; it is a naive denial of the biblical view of humanity.

Just as respect characterizes healthy relationships, binding shame marks unhealthy, codependent relationships. As we turn a corner to explore these shame-based relationships, we again recognize the powerful pull of dysfunctional family patterns.

Shame-based Relationships

If we grew up in shame-based families, we will be drawn to people who repeat the shaming maneuvers we experienced in childhood. These relationships might be humiliating, painful and exhausting, but they are irresistibly familiar. After all, we know the rules to the shame game, so it's easy to play. And this is why most of our relationships have a baffling similarity.

Melody Beattie, author of *Codependent No More*, talks about this attraction to a certain "type." She concluded that, "my type wasn't really my type. He was my 'drug of choice.' " Beattie also reports asking a friend about her latest date. The friend replied, "Oh, you know . . . he's got a different name and face, but essentially he's the same man I have been dating all my life."[1]

In some shame-based, codependent relationships most of the shaming and blatant disrespecting is done by one person, e.g., parent to child, employer to employee. Kristy was in such a codependent relationship with a live-in boyfriend who publicly belittled and privately battered her on a regular basis. When asked why she stayed, Kristy shrugged and said, "I take what I can get; besides it could be lots worse." The "lots worse" Kristy feared was being alone.

Like many other adult children, Kristy is on a lifelong search for a sense of connection to others which provides safety from feelings of abandonment. Kristy does not expect mutual respect in relationships because she had never experienced that as a child. Being connected, however painfully or shame-fully, to someone (anyone!) feels safer than being alone to adults like Kristy who survived childhood abandonment trauma. The greater the perceived abandonment in childhood, the more urgent and desperate is the adult search for safety in connectedness regardless of how much physical, emotional and relational pain is involved.

Mutually Disrespectful Shame-based Relationships

In many codependent relationships, both people shame and deeply disrespect each other, although one person might be less obvious about it.

In an intimate or significant relationship, shamers know where others are most easily hurt and use that information to attack when there is conflict. They specialize in contempt and disdain for the very persons they supposedly love. They attack the independence of their partners by casting doubt on the partner's intelligence, common sense and sanity. They actively seek to lower the other person by emphasizing shortcomings. In short, *shamers diminish the people around them so they can feel better about themselves.*[2]

Yesterday's shamed become today's shamers, as shame begets shame. Blatant shamers might use public humiliation to cement their superiority in the minds of others. Subtle shamers favor rescuing. It allows them to look stronger and more competent than the "victim," while also maintaining the appearance of respectful kindness. Whichever style we choose, it creates problems. And these problems are most clearly seen in the most intimate human relationship: marriage.

Special Challenges of Marriage

Since many of us adult children had unhealthy models of marriage, it isn't surprising that this intense relationship presents special challenges for us to overcome. When most adult children marry, we don't commit to a *romantic partnership* so much as we contract for a *renovation project.* We often undertake complete overhauls of our spouses' personalities even before all the wedding gifts have been unwrapped.

This approach to marriage displays the shame-bound belief which says, "You must look and behave perfectly because you are an extension of me, and you prove that I can connect with a perfect person which will keep others from discovering that I am imperfect."

Marriage and Our Hidden Agendas

Many compulsively codependent adult children approach marriage with hidden agendas. Usually we hide these agendas even from ourselves. All we know is that we have deep, nameless longings in our lives, and we expect our unsuspecting spouses to satisfy them. (But, of course, they have their own longings and agendas.) Our vague feelings that there's something missing in us propels our compulsive drive for personal completion. In marriage, this compulsion is intensified into unspoken demands that our spouses spend their entire lives taking away our childhood pain and filling us with good feelings about ourselves.

It is hard to miss the tragic irony of this codependent approach to relationships in general and marriage in particular. If you have identified with what's been said, you might be one of these adult children who is trying to be filled by another empty person, a "broken cistern" that holds no water. And perhaps you are enabling—even encouraging—others to look to you, another broken cistern, to be filled. God calls this foolish, futile and sinful, for when we pursue broken cisterns to fill inner emptiness, we forsake God, "the spring of living water" (see Jeremiah 2:13). Clearly, marriage tends to magnify the shame-based, codependent relating styles in adult children from dysfunctional families. We see this in the problems we have maintaining healthy personal boundaries.

Codependence and Boundaries

In chapter four we saw that dysfunctional families teach us to be numb to violations of personal boundaries, that sense of where we end and others begin. Healthy personal boundaries are neither too permeable, allowing everything and everyone in, nor impermeable, creating walls around us to keep everything and everyone out.

Because adult children tend to think and live in extremes, we express our codependency with either nonexistent or fortress-like boundaries. The chart in figure 10-1 contrasts healthy boundaries with these two codependent extremes.

Often our shame-based approval addiction and fear of abandonment get in the way of setting healthy boundaries. Many of us are like the adult child from a dysfunctional family who asked me how she could get a married co-worker to leave her alone without getting him angry? She was crushed to learn that she could either set a boundary or try to control his response to her (in this case, by appeasing him), but she could not do both.

Healthy Boundaries and Codependent Extremes

Too Permeable (Inappropriate)	*Permeable* (Appropriate)	*Impermeable* (Inappropriate)
I talk at an intimate level at the first meeting.	I don't overwhelm people with personal information. I allow time for trust to develop.	I don't ever open up, even to people I know to be trustworthy and caring.
I am overwhelmed and preoccupied with a person and his or her needs.	I am able to keep relationships in perspective and function effectively in other areas of my life.	I don't let myself even think about another person I'm interested in.
I can fall in love with a new acquaintance.	I know love is based on respect and trust; these take time to develop.	I don't let loving feelings ever develop for anyone.
I let others determine my reality.	I believe my perceptions are as accurate as anyone's.	I am unwilling to listen to others' perceptions.
I let others direct my life.	I make decisions for myself based on God's leading of my choices.	I refuse to consider the opinions of others.
I don't ever notice when others invade my personal boundaries.	I notice when others try to make decisions for me, are overly helpful, and/or don't consult me about planning my time.	I never allow anyone to help me or give me ideas and suggestions, even when it is helpful and appropriate.
I sacrifice my values if I have to in order to be close to other people.	I am not willing to "do anything" to maintain a relationship. I have biblical values that are not negotiable.	I am never willing to change anything I do to please anybody.

Figure 10-1.

We can't effectively set personal boundaries and at the same time take responsibility for controlling another person's feelings. These acts are mutually exclusive. We set personal boundaries to take care of ourselves, not to control others. In fact, the desire for control will short-circuit our boundary-setting efforts every time. That's bad news for those adult children who are dedicated to controlling others.

Codependency and Controlling Others

Codependents have been called the "fairy godmothers of the world." Now the problem with trying to be everyone's fairy godmother is that you keep waving your magic wand but nothing happens. The truth is this: We do not have the magic power to change and control other people. We are living a fairy tale if we think we do. And living in this fairy tale about control traps us in codependent bondage.

Compulsively codependent adult children inevitably end up being controlled by the very people they attempt to control—just as I got my own finger caught in a mousetrap I was setting for a kitchen marauder. Those of us who most loudly lament our loss of control in unhealthy relationships are usually those who are the most sincerely committed to changing, improving, rescuing, helping (that is to say, controlling) others. In reality, unless you're in a prison, a hostage-taking or other circumstance involving physical duress, one unimpaired adult cannot be the "victim" of another. If you are being controlled and disrespected, you are a *volunteer*, not a *victim*.

For example, adults raised in alcoholically dysfunctional families are often attracted to alcoholics. Many of these adult children endure degrading and even dangerous situations in the name of love as they attempt to save the alcoholic by controlling his or her drinking. Adult children often describe feeling out of control in these relationships. In reality, they have voluntarily relinquished their self-respect and their personal boundaries, along with their control, all because of the erroneous belief that they could—or should—control another adult.

You might be compulsively controlling others because you learned in childhood that you could, and should. Your sense of identity and worth might center on the helping, rescuing relational styles that mark dedicated controllers. Or you might be controlling primarily to reduce the threat of experiencing events that trigger abandonment feelings.

You might take the "strong," over-responsible role and control by rescuing. But even strong-looking rescuers feel inferior inside. They earn the right to exist and be a part of society by saving desperately needy victims. Rescuers have to make themselves indispensable because they believe they are so unimportant.

Perhaps the "weak," under-responsible position of victim might seem more effective for controlling. Those who play this role seem to have given up trying to earn *anything*. They have settled for taking as a way to be connected to all the rescuers who live to give.

Our controlling method is an outgrowth of childhood roles and unrecognized choices to do what makes us feel most safe. Children in dysfunctional families are often forced to play both victim and rescuer. For instance, incest victims are forced to rescue their abusers from legal consequences by keeping the incest a secret. And codependent adults might bounce between victim and rescuer roles in the same or different relationships.

The chart in figure 10-2 summarizes the rescuer and victim styles of controlling relationships in contrast to the non-controlling, responsible position.

Our control methods create relational needs, so rescuers must have victims, and victims always need rescuers. Playing either role is disrespectful and destructive to a relationship. In fact, genuinely trusting, intimate relationships are based on the willingness to give up role-playing.

Codependency, Trust and Intimacy
Adult children have problems with appropriate trusting, and this undermines our efforts to establish genuinely intimate relationships. And, as in most things, we adult children tend to live one of two extreme trusting positions—or bounce back and forth between them.

Anne is a bright, attractive Christian woman who was raised in an incestuous family. Her childhood experiences distorted her concepts of love and sexuality. Anne was convulsed in sobs as she described the relationship with a coworker that left her alone and pregnant.

"I just knew the minute I met him that I could trust him completely.

Personal Responsibility And Codependent Controlling Styles

Weak Victim	Human Adult	Strong Rescuer
(Under-responsible)	(Responsible for Self)	(Over-responsible)
I am so weak I am a "wreck."	I have strengths and weaknesses. I am a human being.	I am so strong I am a "rock."
I have no responsibility for anyone or anything.	I am responsible *for* myself and *to* others.	I am responsible for everything/everyone.
I can't change anybody.	I can change only myself.	I can change everybody.
I need someone to take care of me all the time.	I can take care of myself most of the time. I trust God to care for me at all times.	I will take care of you all the time.
Everything is "too much" for me.	Some things are "too much" for me, but nothing is ever "too much" for God.	Nothing is "too much" for me.
I desperately need you.	I desperately need God, and I long for relationships.	I desperately need to be needed.

Figure 10-2.

He was older than me, and so wise and kind. He said he loved me too and would marry me as soon as he settled some minor personal problems. I never asked the details because I didn't want him to think I didn't trust him. When I told him I was pregnant and would like to get married right away, he laughed and said I was too naive for my own good."

He was right. Anne's inappropriate, immediate overtrusting blinded her judgment. Her "wise and kind" lover already had a wife and family he had no intention of leaving. Overtrusters like Anne use their "blind trust" in a childlike attempt to make the other person trustworthy. Their magical thinking goes something like this: "If I let him see that

I trust him completely, surely he won't want to disappoint and hurt me by proving unworthy of so much trust."

Anne had actually experienced another "family reunion"; her parents had betrayed her trust time and time again. Somewhere, deep inside, adult children like Anne keep hoping that *this time* it will be different. But they unknowingly select the people that guarantee it won't be.

In contrast to Anne's belief in total, automatic, immediate trusting, Daren doesn't trust anyone. Daren's chaotic, abusive childhood convinced him that trusting and being open and vulnerable anytime with anyone always causes pain. Daren uses undertrusting as a shield against the risk of rejection and relational pain. In effect, Daren is convinced that it can *never* be different. And he too unknowingly selects relationships that validate his view.

Can you see that both trusting extremes leave shame-bound adult children feeling isolated and alone? There we stand on one side of the imaginary bridge of broken relationships, hopelessly cut off from having fulfilling relationships with all the "perfect people" on the other side. This confirms our perception that we're different and less than others. This also makes intimacy impossible since intimacy is built on *appropriate* trust.

The Intimacy Challenge

Many adult children like Anne mistake sexual intensity for emotional intimacy. Anne will tell you that intimacy does not mean being sexual and being sexual does not mean being intimate. Anne longed for genuine intimacy, but she settled for a counterfeit pseudo-intimacy that left her alone, pregnant and more shame-bound.

Genuine intimacy is an experience of shared openness. It is the willingness to be who and what we are with another person who is willing to do the same. Clearly, intimacy requires a high degree of trust that both people in the relationship will be psychologically and physically safe.

Trusting is a choice. And appropriate trusting is a reasonable choice based on a person's record of consistent reliability tempered with a realistic understanding of human limitations. People inevitably disappoint and fail each other. God alone deserves our total trust.

Intimacy also requires the risk of mutual self-disclosure. This is a terrifying prospect if we see ourselves as different and less than others. How can we possibly risk taking off our masks of perfection to let our love be without hypocrisy as the apostle Paul advocates in Romans 12:9? If we still believe the lie that our imperfection disqualifies us from loving relationships, we won't risk true intimacy.

Truth releases us from the shame that binds us to these disrespectful, destructive, codependent relational patterns. Changing codependency requires living the truth we are learning, one new choice at a time.

New Choices for Change
A poor peasant lived daily on the verge of starvation. One evening, the old man found a basket of apples on the doorstep of his tiny hovel. Delirious with hunger and joy, he sat down to eat in the light of his one flickering candle. You can imagine his disappointment when he bit into the first apple and found it rotten and wormy. He tossed it aside and tried a second only to find it in the same condition. Again, a third and fourth apple were rotten. Torn by hunger and disgust at what he saw in the apples, the starving peasant paused to consider his choices. Hesitating only a moment, he blew out his candle and ate.

The old peasant eliminated the light to make his desperate choice more bearable. So far you might have gained additional light to see more clearly the quality of your relationships. Some might look pretty rotten. But take heart, we have more options than the starving man in our story did.

His plight actually depicts the limited choices we had as children when we were forced to accept anything given us in order to survive and satisfy our desperate relational hunger. But we are children no more. As adults, we have relational options we did not have as children. However, we must believe and act on this life-changing truth or we will continue to accept rotten relationships that leave us sickened and starving still.

Practicing some of the following choices will change the quality of your relational health—but only if you are in the light so you can see the options clearly.

Healthy Relationship Choices

☐ *Begin by increasing your light by studying and memorizing Bible verses that present principles of healthy relationships.* Psalm 119:130 promises that, "the unfolding of [God's] words gives light; it gives understanding to the simple." Be sure to include the Gospels in your studying; discover for yourself that *Jesus is not codependent.*[3] He didn't invade other's boundaries and his own were well-established (see John 5:6 and Mark 6:31). Jesus didn't make decisions for others and didn't allow them to make his (see Mark 10:17-22 and Matthew 19:13-15). Jesus consistently modeled healthy, respectful relationships.

In your personal notebook or journal, list verses you find that address relationship principles, and write their personal applications. To get you started, here are a few verses from which I've drawn out principles.

1. "If it is possible, as far as it depends on you, live at peace with everyone" (Romans 12:18). Principle: Christians should aim for peaceful relationships. But the phrase, "As far as it depends on you," recognizes the truth that you cannot control the choices of others. Personal Application Example: I want peace with my boyfriend, but I can't control his choices even when I violate my standards to do everything he asks.

2. "Let us therefore make every effort to do what leads to peace and to mutual edification" (Romans 14:19). Principle: Peace is not the only relationship goal. God wants relationships to be balanced and produce mutual growth. Personal Application Example: I think I am the principle caretaker and giver in ninety per cent of my relationships. I am going to look for people who are willing to have more balance and reciprocity in our friendships.

3. "Carry each other's burdens. . . . Each one should carry his own load" (Galatians 6:2 and 5). Principle: Christians are to handle their

normal "loads" with a degree of independence from others, but also be willing to give and receive help in overburdening situations. This is healthy, balanced interdependence. Personal Application Example: I never let friends help me in my overburdened times. I always want to be the wise and strong one. I feel embarrassed and weak when I think about asking someone to help me, yet I am always trying to convince others that it's okay for them to accept my help. I will try to allow others to help me when I need it.

☐ *Begin to discriminate between being responsible* to *and being responsible* for *someone or something.* You are responsible for yourself and the consequences of your own choices. If you are a Christian, you exercise this personal responsibility under the lordship of Christ. And if you have young children, you are responsible for them. But you are not responsible *for* other adults. Mentally competent adults are responsible for themselves and the consequences of their choices.

You do have responsibilities *to* others if you have entered freely chosen relationships involving mutually determined obligations. For example, I am responsible *to* my counselees to be professionally competent, to pray for them and to be on time for our appointments. However, I am not responsible *for* them, their choices or the quality of their lives.

You cannot take responsibility for what you cannot completely control. And you cannot completely control any situation involving the will of another adult. Remember, trying to live the fairy godmother fantasy produces only more shame and a very tired arm from too much wand waving.

☐ *Exercise your freedom to choose by learning to say no.* If you are an approval addict and dedicated rescuer, the word *no* sounds obscene. But if you don't believe you are free to say no, then you never really *choose* to say yes. Unless you recognize and feel free to consider two alternatives in a situation, there is no genuine choice. Most of the time compulsively codependent adult children say yes to anything and everything in a self-protective effort to stay connected to others.

The next time you are asked to do something, consider saying, "I want to think about that before I commit myself." Think and pray about requests for your time. Ask yourself if your desire to say yes is the prompting of the Holy Spirit or the powerful pull of approval addiction.

□ *Allow for the "Law of the Pendulum" as you make new choices.* Recovering codependents are often horrified at how mean they seem to be.

Amy expressed that feeling. "I say no to everybody these days, and one of my friends asked me why I was so mean all of a sudden." Amy had become enamored with the option of saying no. And like most adult children who think in extremes of all-or-nothing, Amy had substituted an automatic no for a compulsive yes. This isn't surprising when you understand the Law of the Pendulum.

Adult children don't undertake change; we declare all-out war. With all-or-nothing thinking, we traffic exclusively in the one and ten positions on a continuum of one to ten. When relinquishing one extreme position, all-or-nothing thinkers tend to swing—like a pendulum—to the opposite extreme before gradually finding an appropriate middle position. This is simply further proof that recovering is a process and that we aren't perfect people. Be patient with yourself and expect that you might be grumpy for awhile as you begin to exercise some new choices.

□ *Identify events and situations that trigger your codependent responses, and practice alternative responses.* For example, Dana wanted to stop spending too much time on the phone playing fairy godmother.

"Every time anyone tells me about a problem, I believe it is my Christian duty to jump in and solve it. I wrote down some of the ideas we talked about in counseling, like just listening, reflecting their feelings and asking about what solutions *they* had thought of. I felt so cruel and uncaring the first few times I tried it. Some of my real 'regulars' kept saying, 'Well what do you think I ought to do, Dana?' But I kept saying it was important for them to come up with their own solutions since it was their problem and their life. You know what? I don't get as many calls as I used to."

☐ *Locate and list your personal boundaries.* The following list was developed by a recovering adult child of an actively alcoholic father.

1. I will no longer tell lies to cover up Dad's alcoholism.

2. I will not allow Dad (or anyone else) to bring alcohol into my home.

3. I will not allow myself or my children to be verbally abused by my parents (or anyone else) even if this means leaving or asking the persons to leave.

4. I will not allow my children to ride in a car when Dad is driving at any time under any circumstances.

5. I will not knowingly rescue other adults from their irresponsible behavior.

6. I will no longer knowingly tolerate emotionally abusive and inappropriate behavior from anyone.

The last two entries on her boundary list were added several months after she established the first four. Participating in a recovery group for adult children helped this woman realize that she needed personal boundaries related to broad codependency issues in addition to those addressing her father's alcoholism. She expects to add others.

☐ *Practice appropriate trusting with the "share-check-share" technique.* This is a helpful choice for both overtrusters and undertrusters. Share-check-share is a safe way to risk the self-disclosure and trusting necessary to develop healthy intimacy. In this process you share a small part of yourself and "check" the other person's response. Is he or she respectful and interested? Then it is probably safe to share more another time. If not, you won't feel totally rejected because you shared only a small part of yourself.[4]

☐ *Identify and use appropriate helpers.* This is actually a multiple-choice choice. First, give yourself permission to be human and to have needs. If you equate human neediness with spiritual or moral weakness, this will be difficult. Second, identify your needs. Do you need a group of other recovering adult children to provide encouragement and support? Do you need professional counseling to work on deep, painful issues concerning your family of origin? I strongly recommend this if you know or suspect that you are an incest survivor. Or perhaps you need a few talks with your pastor or another spiritually sound Christian to deal with distorted views of God.

In the fourth chapter of 2 Timothy, we see a poignant scene in the apostle Paul's life. He is in prison and alone, except for Luke. In verse 9, Paul asks Timothy to come to him quickly. Again in verse 21 he urges Timothy to "get here before winter," after having asked him to bring a cloak (v. 13). Paul was lonely and dreading the cold, dreary winter ahead. Longing for physical and emotional warmth, he sought a cloak and a companion. Paul was not ashamed to ask for either. What an appropriate and healthy response to his felt needs!

Any of these choices will bring positive change for more shame-free, respectful relating. The quality of your current relationships is the sum of thousands of choices made over dozens of years. Your family influenced those past choices, but it does not have to control your current choices—unless you *choose* to let it. You *can* make healthier choices that build healthier relationships.

Personal Reflection

☐ As you consider new choices that will change codependent aspects of your relating style, what seems to be the major obstacle(s)?

☐ Are you willing to reach for healthier relationships rather than cling to the obstacle(s)? If not, what would it take to increase your willingness?

☐ Look at Figure 10-1 on page 136. Star the statements that sound like you. What do the starred statements suggest about your boundaries?

☐ What new choices do you need to practice in order to move to a more healthy, balanced position?

☐ Will you begin practicing any of those new choices? Which one(s)? When?

Looking Ahead

It has been estimated that "fewer than one-third of children born in the 1980s can expect to grow up in two-parent families."[5] As families continue to deteriorate, leaving children with "father-hunger" and other unmet needs, codependency will become a growing relational, emotional and spiritual epidemic.

Many adult children from these families will search for solace in organized (and *dis*organized) religion. And when they do, these bruised and broken believers will bring more than their Bibles to church. They'll bring their shame-bound, distorted concepts of God, themselves and others. Perhaps you already have.

11
Released from Shame-based Concepts of God and Religion

*B*iographers tell us that at two years of age Helen Keller became deaf and blind after a severe illness. This sensory impairment made Helen un- aware of her parents' love during most of her formative years. We are told that her mother stood daily over Helen's crib telling the child of her parents' love for her. Helen's mother lamented that, ". . . [I] cannot make you understand. Your eyes are closed, and your ears are stopped."[1]

I think God, our heavenly parent, must also grieve that so many of us have spiritual ears and eyes that are damaged by the mild or severe abuse we experienced as children in dysfunctional families. I'm sure it comes as no surprise that our relationships with our earthly parents will affect our concept of our heavenly parent. In fact, it's even possible to predict a person's image of God from the type of dysfunction in the person's family. Here are five common distortions of God's character.[2]

□ *"The cruel and capricious God"* is the most extreme distortion of God's true nature. This unbiblical concept of God is the spiritual legacy of adults who repeatedly received brutal, unpredictable abuse in childhood—most often at the hands of their fathers. If you are one of the bruised believers who experienced severe physical and/or sexual abuse as a child, this might be the way you picture God. Is it any wonder you struggle to trust your Father in heaven?

□ *"The demanding and unforgiving God"* seems to be the heavenly parent most often worshiped by Christian adult children of rigid, perfectionistic parents. No matter how much we try, we can never measure up to the demands of this distorted deity who neither forgives nor forgets our failures. When we fall short, watch out. That's when his cruel side is revealed. He seems to take particular delight in sending financial disaster and/or physical disease to underscore his intolerance of spiritual shortcomings. No wonder it is difficult to trust him and experience his love and forgiveness.[3]

□ *"The selective and unfair God"* isn't cruel, capricious, demanding or unforgiving with all Christians—only with those shame-bound adult children who bow before him. While all these distortions are rooted in childhood spiritual abuse by parental authority figures, this false god is the epitome of a shame-shaped deity. This might be the god you serve if you feel that Jesus has revealed himself more fully to other Christians who, in turn, have a deeper relationship with him than you do. Can you see how this misconception captures the sense of being a different-and-less-than Christian?

□ *"The distant and unavailable God"* might care about his worshipers, but he's off somewhere running the universe and can't be bothered with getting too involved in their lives. If your parents were physically and/or emotionally unavailable through prolonged absences, perhaps through death, divorce, illness, military duty or neglect, you might experience God as eternally inaccessible.

☐ *"The kind but confused God"* is a bumbling, benign being rather confused by all the chaos in the world. This might be your distorted deity if you perceived your parents as overwhelmed by the uncontrollable chaos in their lives and in your family.

What happens in dysfunctional families to shape these distortions of God? And how can we solve this serious spiritual problem?

Distorting God's Person

In Psalm 50:21, God identifies the soil in which distortions of his character grow: We think that God is just like human beings. Specifically, we think he is just like our parents.

Parents are our earliest and most influential authority figures. We tend to interpret all other authority figures, human or divine, in their shadows. However, God is *not* just like our parents, no matter how good and godly they were. And he definitely is not just like them if they were significantly impaired.

Equating God with our parents is a natural phenomenon for all children, but if we were raised in a dysfunctional family, this can produce devastating spiritual wounds. In effect, impaired parents cast long, dark shadows in which we might be "caused to stumble" by forming distorted concepts of God.

Unfortunately for Christian adult children, our darkly shadowed distortions don't automatically disappear in the bright light of Christian conversion. They are part of the childish and distorted belief systems we must purposefully choose to put behind us.

Correcting distorted concepts of God is arguably the most important aspect of the lifelong process of mind renewal by which we, as Christians, are being continually transformed. The Moffat translation of Psalm 9:10 suggests the key element in this crucial process. It reads: "Those who know What Thou art can trust in Thee. . . ." Adult children will only be able to trust in God when we know him for who he really is.

It's easy for people used to shame-based relationships to try to have one with God as well. We feel comfortable buying into a human-made system of rules and ritualized works designed to make us acceptable to God. I call this *shame-based religion*. Specifically, I am using this term in contrast to the relationship with God which the Bible presents as the result of faith in the redemptive work of Jesus. This biblical relationship is based on grace—that God chooses to favor us though we have done nothing to deserve his care and can do nothing to earn it.

Like the dysfunctional families they resemble, all shame-based religious systems project expectations that distort and deny truth. In a shame-based *family* system, the expectations for children don't match the truth about child development and human imperfection. In shame-based *religious* systems, expectations of participants don't match the truth of *spiritual* growth and human imperfection. Further, these religious systems distort the truth about God. And if they are shame-based *Christian* religious systems, sincere but problem-laden believers feel different and less than the mythical perfect Christians who are purported to fill the pews. This translates to, "I am the only caterpillar in a butterfly *church*." And this sense of shame leads to perfectionistic pleasing and performing to earn the right to live with, and relate to, God and other Christians. Thus, shame-based churches become extended-family reunions.

Time Out

Stop a moment and ask God to reveal himself to you more fully as he really is. Tell him honestly how you see him now. (Don't worry. You will neither shock nor disappoint him. He already knows.) Ask God to help you use the biblical truths presented in this chapter to lead you out of shame-based religion into a more biblical love relationship with him that is based on the knowledge that he loves and accepts you. He sent his Son to die in order to make that acceptance possible.

Distorting God's Purposes for Christians
In shame-based churches we find many misconceptions about God's

expectations for his children. One of the most pervasive is: "God wants you to be a bondservant to others—serving them from sunup to sundown." I heard a distinguished Christian leader say this in a recent radio sermon. Now *that* is compulsive codependency in a Sunday suit! And it is a distortion of scriptural truth.

In Romans 6:22 we see that Christians have been set free from slavery to sin for the purpose of becoming "slaves to God." The apostle Paul echoes this teaching in Philippians 1:1 (KJV), where he calls himself a bondservant, that is to say, a voluntary slave, of Christ Jesus.

Whose voluntary slave are you? It makes a world of difference to your Christian experience whether you are serving Jesus "from sunup to sundown" or serving others in an attempt to keep everybody happy.

Agape is the New Testament Greek word used to describe the highest kind of love we can express. This is the love that God has for us. Greek scholars have noted that genuine *agape* is more a decision to seek the welfare of others than a sentiment or an emotion.

We won't make everyone happy even if we truly seek each person's welfare. For instance, when we rescue others who seek rescuing, we are likely motivated more by a kind of sloppy *agape* (the desire to avoid experiencing anger and losing relationships) than we are by genuine Christian compassion and *agape*. Their best interests would be better served by allowing them to experience the consequences of their choices. In the name of love, we often rush in to keep someone from experiencing any pain in life. In reality, we might be hurting that person by preventing this friend from facing the sense of personal neediness that God often uses to draw a person to him.

Which relating and serving style sounds like you? Are you performing God-directed ministry or self-protective manipulation? Figure 11-1 contrasts these two styles of Christian service.[4]

Teaching and Living Idolatry

It has been said that your idol or god is whatever gets the most of your time, thought and dependence. We compulsively codependent adult children inadvertently make other people our idols as we look to others

Shame-based vs. God-directed Service

Sanctified Codependency (Self-protective Manipulation)	Compassionate Service (Christ-centered Ministry)
Motivated by self-protection and energized by self-effort.	Motivated and energized by the Holy Spirit of God.
Characterized by legalistic and joyless works.	Characterized by a sense of peace and purpose.
People become statistics or projects to be "won" or "fixed."	People are seen as being the same as I am, needing to be lovingly led to Jesus Christ as Savior and "fixer."
I enjoy serving most when the task is a monumentally big deal.	I enjoy all service to which Christ calls me, even if it appears small.
I demand external validation through public attention and appreciation and become resentful if I go unnoticed.	I can accept attention, but I don't demand it; I can remain unnoticed without growing resentful.
Serving is a source of my identity and sense of worth in the church.	My service is the outgrowth of an identity based on being a loved, redeemed bearer of God's image.
In the name of "Christian love," I bail out others, not expecting them to take personal responsibility for themselves.	I take responsibility for myself under Christ's lordship and let go of others to do the same.
I jump in and *take* care of others without waiting to be asked.	I *give* help appropriately when asked (emergencies excepted).
As the "server," I feel and appear competent and powerful (like a savior). The "servee" feels and appears incompetent and weak (like a victim).	"Server" and "servee" have attitudes of mutual respect whereby neither feels nor appears incompetent, for we both realize our roles might be reversed next time.
I use my busyness for God to numb painful feelings and distract me from unmanageable parts of my life.	My active serving is balanced with quiet times of prayer, Bible study and meditation on Scripture, when I reflect on my total lifestyle.
I often feel burned out and bitter because I don't take care of my health and I'm unable to set limits.	I can say no to requests of others for I recognize my own limitations and need for healthy self-care.

Figure 11-1.

to provide the security and significance that can be found only in a personal relationship with God. Such idol worship has two contradictory expressions: playing God for others and looking to others to play God for us.

We adult children frequently "play God" in the lives of others by believing that it is up to us and us alone to bring meaning, happiness and direction to some poor, miserable and misguided sinner.

As we perform our impressions of God for this person, we are operating from a "my will be done" stance. We usually become increasingly absorbed with the other's needs while totally ignoring our own. Think about what this conveys. We project ourselves as beings who can meet all the needs of others and yet have no unmet needs of our own. In other words, we are both all-sufficient and self-sustaining. Those are attributes of God, not humans.

Curiously, even if we impersonate God for others, we might also look to them to play deity for us. It is as if we say, "I will play God for you by keeping you safe from any painful feelings of abandonment and by providing your sense of identity and worth, and I expect you to do the same thing for me."

This I'll-Be-God-for-You-and-You-Be-God-for-Me relational style is not Christian love; it is codependency. It is also what we learn in most dysfunctional families.

In well-functioning families, children do not have to perform the role of all-sufficient, self-sustaining emotional provider to their parents. But you might have been thrust into that responsibility at an early age. Because you live what you learn, you might have continued to play the god-role for others. In fact, rescuing others might be the core of your identity. Many adult children have no sense of who they are apart from the defensive childhood roles they had to play.

No wonder we automatically take our rescuing lifestyles right to church if we are Christians. And no wonder we might have problems understanding God's purposes for our lives. Shame-based service is merely rescuing in religious robes. Often, it will be welcomed with open arms.

"So, what's the problem," you ask? "At least the jobs are getting done at church!"

There are at least three problems with this. The problems are related to the issue of God's purposes for his children.

□ *Problem 1: Shame-based service depends on looking at people instead of at God.* First, there is the question of whose slaves we are. We will always fix our eyes on the one(s) we serve. If we are serving for the approval of others to gain a sense of identity and worth and to feel safe from abandonment, we will inevitably focus on people. And we will always be in danger of loving the approval of others more than the approval of God. (See John 12:43.) When that occurs, the emphasis in our spiritual lives will be solely external—sort of an "anointed appearance management."

In contrast, Hebrews 12:2 tells Christians that we are to "fix our eyes on Jesus." If we do, we will respond as quickly to the leading of his Spirit when he calls us to quiet times of spiritual refreshing in solitary meditation as we do when he directs us to busy days of active serving in public ministry. If our eyes are on others, we will never risk the frowns that come when we periodically give up "active service" for time alone with God.

This internal, Godward focus on *being* rather than *doing* is the antithesis of the shame-based beliefs we learned in our dysfunctional families. And those are the beliefs that shaped our concepts of self. I've had many adult children tell me they can't work quiet times with Jesus into their schedules because they are too busy "serving others."

□ *Problem 2: Shame-based service occurs when we misunderstand self-denial.* Many Christian churches are fond of preaching "self-denial." They exposit Christ's call to deny self and take up a cross (in Matthew 16:24) as a directive to give up smoking, dancing, gossiping, and other taboos, and take up as many church-related responsibilities as possible. Though Christ does warn against loving the "things of the world" more than we love him (1 John 2:15), a closer look at Matthew 16:24 reveals a deeper, infinitely more life-altering command.

The Greek word translated as the word *deny* means to turn away from or say no to a *person*, not to a thing. It also has the idea of formerly having been loyal or obedient to that person you are now choosing to deny.[5] In Matthew 16:24, Jesus doesn't tell us to deny our *practices;* he calls us to deny our *personalities*—our basic concepts of self. This requires laying aside old thinking patterns.

☐ *Problem 3: Shame-based service occurs when we live transferred rather than transformed lives.* One of God's purposes for his children is that we renounce our loyalties and obedience to the ideas that shaped us and move into the "renewed" thinking that promotes our transformation processes. (See Romans 12:1-2.) A major piece of our old thinking includes the beliefs that shaped our personalities and concepts of self.

As Christian adult children, we might have settled for *transferred* lives instead of *transformed* lives. We might have simply transferred all the compulsively codependent thinking and relating from our dysfunctional families into our church families. God wants to bring us out of that painful, shame-full way of thinking and living. And this is where mind renewal and self-denial embrace. Part of denying ourselves means denying the old thinking patterns that molded us.

In this continuous, lifelong process, we shift our loyalties and obedience from the world and family rules to Christ and his truth. This sets us free to receive God's gift of a new concept of ourselves based on grace.

Whether we function as rescuers or as victims, we could lay aside self-protective maneuvers and find identity and worth in our relationships with God. We could experience the freedom that comes from knowing that we don't serve *for* a position of acceptance but *from* a position of acceptance.

This process would bring both balance and wholeness to individual Christians as well as to the entire church. And both are sorely needed in shame-based churches that distort God's purposes.

Distorting God's Purposes for Churches
In order to move in the direction of wholeness and balance, we need to be in churches that nurture these attributes. Such congregations are

committed to learning to be real about themselves, their pain and their joy as they seek to make Jesus more and more the Lord of their lives.

If you are a Christian adult raised in a dysfunctional family, the chances are good, however, that you've been (and may still be) involved in at least one church or parachurch ministry rooted in shame. After all, you feel comfortable functioning in shame-based systems; you were raised in one.

As always, we need to recognize a problem before we can change it. How can we distinguish shame-based churches from those that are truly grace-full? The chart in figure 11-2 summarizes expectations and experiences typical of these different systems. Why not use the chart to assess your current church or parachurch organization?

How tragic that many Christians, released from biblical shame by God's grace, sit in Bible-believing churches hearing binding-shame preached as "good news."

Early in his ministry, Jesus announced that he came to bring "good news," that is to say, the gospel, to certain people he vividly pictured. Jesus' portrait gives us God's perspective on the type of people with whom he builds churches. Perhaps you'll see yourself in his words.

The Spirit of the Lord is on me, because he has anointed me to preach good news to the poor. He sent me to proclaim freedom for the prisoners and recovery of sight for the blind, to release the oppressed, to proclaim the year of the Lord's favor. (Luke 4:18-19)

Isn't that amazing? God expects churches to be filled with the spiritually and personally poor, the bound, the blind and the oppressed. That is a picture of complete brokenness! As broken people, we need a place that gives us hope for healing and guidance toward wholeness.

Churches that have God's perspective function as "therapeutic communities." No one is surprised that Christians have serious problems; there are programs in place to help solve them.

Shame-based churches do not function as therapeutic communities because they believe that God expects a different kind of person to populate the pews. Instead of the bankrupt, the bound, the blind and the bruised, shame-based churches want to project the image of being

Shame-based vs. Grace-based Church Families

Shame-full Church Family	*Grace-full Church Family*
Rooted in shame-based religionism; keeping human-made rules in order to be "right."	Rooted in grace-based relationship; trusting in Christ's death and resurrection in order to be "right."
God is experienced as a demanding Shepherd who drives his sheep.	God is experienced as an understanding Shepherd who leads his sheep.
I am expected to be totally (or almost totally) transformed the moment I trust Christ.	I am expected to keep on being transformed by having my mind renewed as long as I live.
Since I should be totally transformed (perfect) I am a different-and-less-than Christian because I'm not perfect.	Since I am in a lifelong process of being transformed to be like Jesus, my imperfections don't surprise me, church members or God.
Members with obvious problems are an embarrassment to the church. Since real Christians have no serious problems, no provisions have been made to help.	Members with obvious problems are expected since the past and present effects of sin in Christians' lives can cause serious problems. There are programs in place to provide appropriate help.
Small-group Bible studies are dangerous places because someone might get close enough to see behind my mask of perfection and know I have problems.	Small-group Bible studies are safe places to practice being maskless and be with others who do the same. It's great to go where I don't have to hide my problems.
Emphasis is on looking religious by wearing the right clothes and carrying the right translation of the Bible.	Emphasis is on developing a deeper relationship of love and trusting obedience with Jesus Christ.
Emphasis is on performance.	Emphasis is on worshiping God.
Emphasis is on revealing and rebuking sinners.	Emphasis is on restoring repentant sinners.
Attendance at church activities is used as the main indicator of a person's true spirituality.	Acknowledgment that true spirituality is reflected in total lifestyle and known only to God.

Figure 11-2.

filled with the prosperous, the prestigious, the pretty and the problem-free. They don't want broken people. They want perfect people.

Did you hear about the patient at Mt. Carmel Mercy Hospital in Detroit who was shot dead as he lay in his hospital bed recovering from a previous gunshot wound?

A hospital staff person said that the victim had been listed in fair condition prior to the [second] shooting and was looking forward to going home. Hospital patients and employees were stunned. A spokes-person said that nothing like this had happened in 50 years of the hospital's existence.[6]

I'd say that that hospital (with only one shooting in fifty years) was a pretty safe place compared to some shame-based churches that regularly shoot their wounded members! Shooting the wounded makes sense if churches are supposed to be filled with perfect people. In such churches, problems are an intolerable embarrassment and must be denied, even if it means destroying bruised and broken believers in the process. (Remember, all dysfunctional families are committed to appearance management—dysfunctional *church* families included.)

What a distortion of God's purposes for his church! The body of Christ is meant to be a fellowship of sin-broken believers in the process of being restored to wholeness. The fact that you are not a perfect person or a totally transformed Christian does not make you "different-and-less-than." To some degree, *all* of us Christians struggle with the effects of past and present sin in our lives. Try to find a church that accepts this truth.

New Choices for Change

Nowhere is truth more important as the basis for new choices than when you practice changing shame-based concepts of God and religion. Fortunately, the Scriptures contain truth about God's person and his purposes for believers, both individually and corporately.

The following suggestions will help you get started practicing new choices.[7]

☐ *Choose to see God as he is revealed in Scripture instead of as someone made in your parents' image.* You do this by learning about the general attributes of God and by focusing on his parental qualities. Here are some ways to do that.

1. Do a Bible study on the general attributes of God. Someone has said that the spiritual question of childhood is: Will God be able to love me? But the spiritual question adults ask is: Will I be able to love God? Learning to see him as he is revealed in Scripture will enable you to replace distorted concepts of God with the truth. In turn, this will help you love and trust God more. To get you started, Appendix C lists some of God's attributes. In addition, there are Bible-study guides available to help you.[8]

2. Using a concordance to help you, do a Bible study on the parental and maternal attributes of God. For instance, God as a father is compassionate and understanding (Psalm 103:13-14) and loving and forgiving (Luke 15:11-31). God as a mother is concerned and comforting (Isaiah 66:13) and totally focused on helpless children (Isaiah 49:14-16). Note that some verses directly contrast God with human parents. For example, Psalm 27:10 declares that if your own parents forsake you, God will take you up. And Hebrews 13:5 says God will never forsake you.

3. Be creative as you read and study. Remember, you are practicing your choice to see God as he really is. For example, in 1 John 4:8 you find the statement that "God is love." That's wonderful, but what does that mean to you as you seek to see God as a heavenly parent very different from your earthly parents? Figure 11-3 shows a creative application of 1 Corinthians 13:4-8 to the truth that God is love.[9]

4. Read books about the attributes of God. Two of the classics are *Knowing God* by J. I. Packer and *The Knowledge of the Holy* by A. W. Tozer. Your Christian bookstore would have additional selections.

□ *Write out your thoughts and feelings about what you are learning.* Use your personal journal to record your observations about how God differs from your previous, parent-shaped perceptions of him. Also write personal applications for your new truth about God's character. This is an example of such an application written by a recovering

My Heavenly Father

My heavenly Father is very patient and kind.
My heavenly Father is neither envious nor boastful.
My heavenly Father is not arrogant.
My heavenly Father is neither rude nor self-seeking.
My heavenly Father is not quick to take offense.
My heavenly Father keeps no score of my forgiven sins.
My heavenly Father does not gloat over my sins,
    but always delights when I choose truth.
My heavenly Father knows no limit to his endurance, no end to his trust.
My heavenly Father is always hopeful and patient.
My heavenly Father's good purposes never fail.

Figure 11-3.

Christian adult child of rigidly perfectionistic parents.

I am blown away by Jesus' description of the father in the "Prodigal Son" parable. He is entirely different from my dad. I have been afraid and very reluctant to confess my sins to God because I always pictured Him with His arms folded over His chest, shaking His head back and forth and with a disgusted look on His face—just like my dad. I think I can pray more easily if I can hold onto the picture of God as loving and forgiving.

☐ *Admit your anger and disappointment with God.* This will not come as a shock to God! But it might come as a shock to you that Christians can have those feelings. Adult children often struggle to separate the physical reality of this world from spiritual reality. Perhaps your reasoning has gone something like this: If God is kind and just, then life ought to be kind and just. The flip side of this is: Since life has been unfair and cruel to me, God must be unfair and cruel.

When God gave that awesome gift of choice to humans, it even included the choice to neglect and abuse children. You might have been a victim of such choices. God understands and grieves for your pain. He is not angry when you cry, "Why?" or "Why me?" or "Why again?" (Remember, he is different from your parents.)

There are no easy answers for why the sovereign, loving God of the universe has chosen to let sin run its destructive course. Philip Yancey has pondered this question and concluded that Calvary's cross revealed the world for the breeding ground of violence and injustice it really is. But God's plans weren't completed on Good Friday.

Good Friday demolished the instinctive belief that this life is supposed to be fair. But Easter Sunday gives a bright and startling clue to the riddle of the universe. Someday, God will restore the physical reality of planet Earth to its proper place under his reign. The miracle of Easter will be enlarged to cosmic scale. It is a good thing to remember, when disappointment with God hits, that we live out our days on Easter Saturday.[10]

And it is good to choose, as you are being released from shame, to be honest about your natural, human feelings of anger and disappointment at the Easter Saturday struggles you experience.

☐ *Choose to trust God.* Earlier I said that trusting is a choice, and appropriate trust is a choice based on a record of consistent reliability. If your parents were not consistently reliable, and if you have been victimized by sinful choices, it might be extremely difficult for you to trust God. You might have been assuming he is just like your folks and you've probably been blaming him for all your pain.

I am inviting you to make a new choice for change by consciously deciding to trust God after examining his record of reliability and faithfulness in the Bible. But you need to be clear about what you can appropriately trust him for. *You cannot trust God for a pain-free life in this sin-stained world.* But you can trust him to comfort and strengthen you in your pain. If you are willing to practice this choice, tell God and ask him to empower you.

☐ *Choose your church family.* As a child, you could not choose the family in which you were raised, but now you *can* choose your church family. By this I mean that you can *deliberately* evaluate your church's "spiritual health" and decide if you should stay. It *is* possible to find churches that balance both the grace and truth Jesus came to bring (see John 1:17). I know, because I am in one. Ask God to lead you in this.

☐ *Evaluate your current relationship with God.* Dr. Raymond Dupont has suggested that believers live in one of three relationships with God in their Christianity. Each reflects a response to the clear biblical call to love and obey God.

One relationship where many Christians get stuck is the "have to" response. "I *have to* obey God because my relationship with him is based on my law-keeping and good works." This is commonly called legalism. In Galatians, Paul had some pretty strong things to say about this approach to Christianity.

Some of us get so burdened down and burned out in legalistic, shame-based churches, we swing over to a lawless, do-our-own-thing lifestyle. But as God's children, we will be miserable in sin and will eventually return to obedience. At that point, we might move into the "need to" response. "I *need to* obey God because the alternative is so destructive to me and to others."

To understand the third response, you need to know that all the responses are not dependent on how much we love God but on the degree to which we experience God's love for *us*. Only Christians who personally experience God's gracious love for them will move into the "want to" response to obedience. "I *want to* obey God because I am overwhelmed with his love for me."

As you begin to learn what God is really like, as you find a grace-based church family who will help you learn to serve God in positive ways and as you ask God to empower you to trust him further, you will increasingly experience God's gracious love for you. In the process, you'll be released from shame more and more.

Personal Reflection

If you've established your relationship with God by asking Jesus into your life, try to determine where you are in your relationship with God according to Dr. Dupont's three responses. Where would you like to be?

☐ As you look over the suggested choices for change, which one(s) will you begin practicing to move toward your goal? How will you start?

☐ When will you begin?

Looking Ahead

If you are like me, you probably look at chapter titles in the table of contents before you start reading a book. In that case, you knew that eventually I would get around to *that* topic—forgiveness.

You might be one of those adult children who is a long way from the "want to" response when it comes to thinking about forgiveness. That's okay. Hang in and read on, even if "have to" is all you can muster.

12
Released to Forgive the Shamers

T *his is a "wimp book."*

And this is the wimpiest chapter because, according to the writer of a recent parent-bashing book, therapist/authors who encourage forgiveness are writing "wimp books." That therapist/author stated: "Forgiveness is another form of denial. Forgiveness is so phony, it gives people an excuse to not work hard at change."[1]

If you think that forgiving is "wimpy" denial, you have the wrong idea about genuine, biblical forgiveness. Forgiving is hard work, and it is costly. As we examine the reasons for the problems with and the principles of forgiveness, I hope you will be challenged to consider that its high cost is unquestionably exceeded by its rich benefits.

Reasons to Forgive

We may have different motives each time we choose to forgive someone. Here are three important reasons for Christian adult children to forgive.

First, we have been born into God's family by his grace. And, according to Ephesians 4:23, 32, we start to look like our heavenly Father when we practice kindness, compassion and forgiveness. And when we become more like the Father, we will benefit our own earthly families. This is another compelling reason to forgive.

Danny was working hard to forgive his parents for the physical and emotional neglect he experienced as a child in an alcoholic family. He was motivated, in part, by a desire to model new patterns of forgiveness for his own children. In therapy he had come to believe in the Adult Child's Golden Rule, which states: Live in such a way that you can expect the same amount of love, acceptance and forgiveness from your children as you showed your own parents.[2]

Danny explained, "My folks never let go of grudges against their parents. They displayed them proudly like badges of courage. I always thought that was just how families were supposed to be. I know I've really messed up as a dad, and I sure need my kids to forgive me. So I thought I'd better start showing them it's possible."

Danny hopes that the new, forgiving approach to family relationships will help his children release their troubled pasts and move on with their lives.

A third reason to forgive is that forgiveness allows us to focus on the future rather than the past. It is motivated by saying, "I've replayed the hurt and rekindled the hatred long enough! I won't remain impaled on the barbed wire of bitterness one day longer!"

Forgiving means releasing our dreams of a better *yesterday* so we can reach for the reality of a better *tomorrow*. This is one of forgiveness' most hopeful purposes, but it also raises one of the problems we can have with forgiveness.

Problems with Forgiveness

Forgiving is an admission that something hurtful *really* happened. As one incest survivor explained, "If I begin to work on forgiveness, then

I am actually saying that this is not all just in my head."

Time Out

Stop a moment, and listen to your thoughts. You may be saying to yourself, "There's no way on God's green earth this woman understands what she's asking when she talks to me about forgiving." And, of course, you're right. I can't know your particular pain. But I know mine, and I have seen a lot of other adult children's unbelievable pain. Yes, it is extremely difficult to face past hurts and feel past hurts so that you can forgive the hurters. But unforgiveness is worse! You give your hurters the power to continue hurting you.

Please, ask God to open your heart and mind to a fresh consideration of forgiveness as you read on. I'll be honest about the cost of forgiving. Will you be honest about your need to experience the benefits of forgiving?

In effect, forgiving validates the reality of our painful pasts. And this reactivates old, painful feelings while bringing additional anguish of its own. Clearly, validating betrayals of trust, great or small, and increasing emotional pain are two significant problems with forgiveness. But there are others, and they all involve misunderstandings about the nature of forgiveness.

Misunderstandings about Forgiveness

The major misunderstanding about forgiveness concerns the messages it sends. These misunderstandings create a stumbling block that prevents many adult children from seriously considering forgiveness. Here are the three misunderstandings about forgiving that produce most forgiveness "drop-outs."

☐ *Misunderstanding #1: Forgiving means nothing ever happened or that it was "no big deal."* Nothing could be further from the truth! Is that what God says about our sin when he forgives? On the contrary, it is precisely because our sin did happen and because sin is such a colossal "big deal" that it needs to be forgiven. Excusing, minimizing, trivializing it won't work. It must be forgiven—not denied or discounted.

☐ *Misunderstanding #2: Forgiving means automatic, instant, unlimited reconciliation.* Forgiveness is a prerequisite to reconciliation, but they are not synonymous. Again, the biblical pattern is instructive. The biblical basis for reconciliation is mutual acceptance of truth. . . .

> Without an individual being willing to agree with God, there is no mutual acceptance of truth and no basis for reconciliation. It could be said that God offers the possibility of reconciliation to all; but possession of reconciliation is limited to those who agree with God's truth about their need of it.[3]

The erroneous belief that forgiving automatically necessitates immediate, no-holds-barred reconciliation leaves us with two equally unacceptable options if we face the challenge of forgiving adults who are still actively abusive. First, we would have to open ourselves and our children to further abuse. This option is not fair for us or our children, and it also promotes the abuser's sinning. Giving the abuser opportunities to go on abusing would clearly violate the teaching of Ephesians 5:11 which tells Christians to "have nothing to do with the fruitless deeds of darkness, but rather expose them."

Our second option is equally unacceptable: postponing forgiveness until the actively abusing shamers accept the truth about their harmful actions and get help to change. The problem here is they may never get help. This option leaves us in bondage to the shamer's abuse and to our unforgiveness.

Forgiveness is unrestrainable and unilateral. Nothing can ever stop us from forgiving anyone at any time. But the other person(s) can block unlimited reconciliation by denying the truth. Though forgiveness and reconciliation are closely related, they are not the same.

For adult children, this means that even when we have sincerely chosen to forgive, we may need to settle for very limited reconciliation with some people. Their emotional problems and/or lifestyle choices may preclude anything more.

For example, Belinda is a recovering Christian adult child who has forgiven her emotionally and physically abusive father. During her parents' recent visit to her home, Belinda's three-year-old son fell and hurt his head. Later, her father, who always frightens the boy, tried to get his grandson to come to him. When the child hesitated, Belinda's father said, "If you don't come here, I'll hit you right where your head hurts."

"I couldn't believe my ears," Belinda told me. "I was so shocked and angry I couldn't speak. I grabbed Billy and carried him into his room to stop his crying and comfort him. After calming us both down, I came out and asked my folks to leave. They honestly seemed surprised that I was 'getting so hysterical over nothing,' as they put it. I determined that day that I would never, ever leave my child alone with my folks. My dad hasn't changed, and my mom still won't protect children from him. I have forgiven my mom and dad for their abuse in my childhood, but I don't think God expects me to ignore what is still going on."

I think Belinda has made a wise decision. *Opening your heart to forgive does not mean closing your eyes to abuse.* We don't have to wait to forgive until limits are unnecessary. Forgiveness and boundary setting are *not* mutually exclusive.

□ *Misunderstanding #3: Forgiving means never having any painful memories or emotions related to the hurts or the hurters.* People who use all-or-nothing thinking tend to assume that forgiveness must either be an event or a process. Forgiveness is both. Forgiving begins with an initial, purposeful commitment of our wills in which we "set sail" for forgiveness. But even after sincere commitments, we can be blown temporarily off course by painful memories or other violent emotional storms. During these storms we may feel confused, discouraged and/or guilty if we misunderstand the nature of forgiveness. It's important to remember that only God forgives perfectly. The rest of us have to keep working at it with continual recommitment.

Belinda knew about the "setting-your-sail-for-forgiveness" metaphor and that helped her understand her emotional distress and her struggle to forgive.

"Hearing my dad threaten my son and seeing my mother just stand there doing nothing brought back a flood of memories and feelings. Talk about being 'blown off course'! I was really a mess for a couple of days. But I kept remembering that forgiving was a recommitment process, and I asked the Lord to give me the grace to keep on doing it."

Clarifying these three misunderstandings about the nature of forgiveness has been helpful as Belinda continues to recommit to her goal of forgiving her impaired parents.

The Principles of Forgiveness

One of Scripture's most encouraging examples of forgiveness is found in the Genesis account of Joseph's life. You probably remember the story. Joseph was the pampered son of a wealthy father. As a teen, Joseph didn't use very good judgment when he told his older brothers about dreams of ruling over them. So, fed up with their father's favoritism and Joseph's boasting, they decided to kill him. After one brother convinced them not to kill Joseph, they spared him, selling him into slavery instead.

In Egypt, Joseph landed in prison for maintaining high moral standards in a low moral environment. Eventually God raised him to a position of authority second only to Pharaoh. Decades later, during a severe famine, the brothers came to Egypt to buy grain. They didn't recognize Joseph, but he knew them instantly. Joseph had a chance to settle the score.

Joseph chose to forgive his brothers and arrange for them, their households, and his father to settle in one of the best sections of Egypt. But the brothers were still uncertain about the sincerity of Joseph's forgiveness, and they feared he would take his revenge after their father's death. In fear and remorse, they threw themselves at Joseph's feet and declared they were his slaves. In one of the most intensely emotional scenes on the pages of Scripture, Joseph assured them that they were safe and he would generously provide for them.

Joseph demonstrated the first principle of forgiveness.

☐ *Principle #1: Forgiveness is a realistic view of the hurt and hurters.* In

Genesis 50:20, Joseph bluntly declares, "You intended to harm me. . . ." How's that for a realistic view?

Joseph might have blamed his own immaturity or his father's tactless favoritism, but he didn't. Instead, he put the responsibility squarely where it belonged: on his brothers' sinful choices.

Surely, a realistic view includes attributing responsibility to the hurters. This is an obvious truth, but one that abuse survivors often struggle to assimilate. As noted in previous chapters, children blame themselves for even the most brutal abuse rather than acknowledge that they were totally powerless to control their abusers' choices. This phenomenon makes it difficult for adult children to take a realistic view of the hurt and hurters.

A realistic view of the hurt and hurters also includes placing both in the context of intergenerational family patterns. However, understanding the hurters is not an invitation to excuse the hurt. *Understanding a sinful choice does not make it right or acceptable.* And understanding more does not mean you have less to forgive.

Belinda learned that too.

"I was horrified when I found out about how my dad was raised. His whole family was so violent. He had three older brothers and a father who beat him up almost daily. I know none of this excuses the decisions he made about how to treat me and my sister, but somehow it helped me be more willing to forgive him. And it increased my circle of forgiveness. I mean I also forgave my grandfather too."

Attempting to understand why persons hurt us in the past may facilitate forgiving and broaden our spheres of forgiveness, just as it did for Belinda. But no amount of understanding will eliminate the need to cancel debts.

☐ *Principle #2: Forgiveness is releasing the right to get even.* Here is where forgiving can feel unfair, for there seems to be a universal human desire to balance the scales of right and wrong. You may be struggling with this as did Janie, the adult daughter of an emotionally abusive mother and sexually abusive stepfather.

"Wait a minute, if I just forgive my folks, they won't get what's coming to them and neither will I," Janie exclaimed. "It's not fair for me to be hurt over and over without somebody admitting it or having to pay. At the very least, they ought to admit they were wrong and say they're sorry. If they would just say, 'I'm sorry' it would be easier."

Easier perhaps, but would an apology pay for repeated betrayals of trust? In fact, ask yourself, what could those hurters and shamers in your past possibly ever do to make up for what happened? In effect, they owe a debt—large or small—which they can never repay.

Can you see the picture? There they are, standing in front of you with empty hands and empty pockets, utterly unable to pay for the past. And there you are facing a choice that will shape your future. You can continue trying to collect the debts they rightfully owe you by exacting verbal and nonverbal tolls. But this means you must constantly replay the past to keep their deficit balance fresh in your mind. Or you can cancel the debt. I didn't say deny the debt, but *cancel* it.

We will resist this suggestion if we believe it releases our abusers and shamers from responsibility for their past choices and lets them off the hook. But that is not what forgiving does. It releases *us* from *our* bondage to *their* past choices. The tragic irony is that while we keep our hurters imprisoned in hatred, we remain in bondage to bitterness and unforgiveness. This has devastating impact on every area of our lives, including our physical well-being. A physician named Arnold Fox has concluded that:

> Forgiveness is a gift to yourself. . . . Forgiveness allows your body to turn down the manufacture of those chemicals which are tearing you apart, body and soul. Doctors can give you all sorts of medicines for your headaches, your heart, your stomach pains, your spastic colon, your anxiety and other problems. But the medicines will not get to the root of the problem: "Unforgiveness." The cure for that lies in forgiving. When you savor your hatred, your anger and rage, you don't hurt "them," you hurt yourself. The bottom line is that we can forgive and get on with our lives.[4]

Forgiving also includes acknowledging the reality that "they" are as bankrupt before us as we are before God. And forgiving is taking the issue of the hurter's unpayable sin debts and handing it to God to settle. Isn't that what we had to do with *our* unpayable sin debts?

One of the primary meanings of the Greek word translated "forgive" in the New Testament is to completely cancel a debt.[5] In earlier chapters, we saw that Jesus' death paid the sin debt for all who would believe. And this debt includes the shamers' sins against us. Our desires to have the scales balanced are realized at the cross. We are free to stop collecting debts our parents or others owe but can never repay. We can release the past into God's hands and, in turn, be released for a future of greater emotional freedom.

Joseph is a good example of this. His brothers were relieved and surprised when he told them, " 'Don't be afraid. I will provide for you and your children.' And he reassured them and spoke kindly to them" (Genesis 50:21). They feared justice, but found grace.

It has been said that justice is getting what we deserve, and mercy is not getting what we deserve. But grace is getting what we don't deserve. As Christians, we have received grace from God. And when he exhorts us to forgive as we've been forgiven, God is asking us to grace us as we've been graced.

Now the problem is that we can't do that operating in our own strength, which brings us to the third forgiveness principle.

☐ *Principle #3: Forgiveness requires admitting that forgiving is not merely difficult; it is humanly impossible.* Forgiving is not natural to human beings. We are more in tune with an "eye for an eye and a tooth for a tooth." As a result, many of us go through our lives and our relationships blind and toothless!

We blind and toothless Christians operate from a double standard when it comes to grace. We enjoy relating to *God* by *grace*, but we insist on relating to *others* by *law*. This is particularly true if we are adult children, because most dysfunctional families specialize in grudges, not grace. So how are we adult children going to learn to forgive and release the past?

Again, Joseph's story offers a clue. In Genesis 41:51, Joseph credits God with enabling him to change his perspective on his brothers' murderous cruelty and the subsequent years of slavery. It wasn't that Joseph was a superhuman saint; he worshiped a supernatural God.

God is not playing games with us about forgiveness. He doesn't call us to forgive without supplying the power to do it, and he has provided the indwelling Holy Spirit to empower this humanly impossible task.

The Need to Forgive Ourselves
Often we adult children seem to need this supernatural empowerment *most* when it comes to forgiving ourselves. My client Marcia had this difficulty. I vividly recall the day she tried to convince me she didn't deserve God's forgiveness.

"But you don't understand. . . ." Marcia's words were swept away by a wave of body-wrenching sobs as she buried her face in her hands. Several minutes went by before she could speak again.

"What I haven't made clear is that. . . ." Her voice broke again as she struggled to choke back her tears. ". . . I was a Christian when all this happened."

Marcia had described several years of sexual promiscuity that included an affair with her married boss and an abortion. An adult child from a divorced and dysfunctional home, Marcia had reached out to fill her "father hunger" and settled for relational garbage. She was consumed with self-hatred and believed God was so disappointed in her that he'd turned his back on her.

Marcia's response to her sinful behavior isn't surprising. For Christian adults from dysfunctional families, our post-salvation sins may be the ones that haunt us most. Though we can't disappoint God (his expectations are always realistic), we can grieve him. He knows how destructive the results of our sin will be in our lives and in the lives of others.

But in spite of the grief we cause him, he chose to give us life and to love us even though he knew everything we would ever do and everything others would ever do to us.

Marcia finally accepted God's gracious forgiveness, and she forgave herself. Marcia also learned that confessing her sins was no substitute for forsaking them, so she began to build healthier relationships. One step in forgiving herself was rejoining the choir. Marcia had always loved singing, but to "help" God in punishing her she had dropped out of choir and other activities that brought her joy.

Do you "help" God by punishing yourself for past, forsaken sins? You may have confessed your haunting, past sins and turned from them. But have you confessed your complete forgiveness? *Confess* literally means to "agree with" or "say the same thing."[6] Perhaps you can quote 1 John 1:9, "If we confess our sins, he is faithful and just and will forgive us our sins and purify us from all unrighteousness." But do you believe it? I mean, do you believe it for *you?* Have you said the same thing God says about your confessed sins? He says, "They are forgiven!"

God has canceled our sin debts and released us from the need to try to punish ourselves. When we *continue* to punish ourselves, we are making a mockery of the cross and God's promise to forgive his children.

It's true that I don't know how horrible your sin might be. But I know how great God's grace is. And I know that either "the blood of Jesus, his Son, purifies us from all sin," (1 John 1:7) or God is a liar. *"All* sin" includes even yours—and mine.

As we are increasingly able to experience God's forgiveness and grace, we will be increasingly released to forgive our hurters and shamers—even ourselves.

New Choices for Change

Jesus' promise that truth sets us free is gloriously realized in the lives of those who receive God's grace and choose to grace others. Remember, your choice is mutual release or mutual bondage. The following suggestions are just a few of the new choices available to help you change from patterns of unforgiveness and bondage to patterns of grace and freedom.

☐ *Don't rush into a counterfeit, "cheap" forgiveness.* After an entire chapter of telling you how important it is to forgive your hurters and shamers, now I am suggesting that you take your time. You may be inclined to toss out a quick, thick "blanket forgiveness" to cover all the pain of your past. But that is not genuine, biblical forgiveness. True forgiveness is costly. It was for God, and it will be for you. You need to face and feel the hurts before you are ready to forgive.

You may want to commit to forgive at the start of your recovering process even though you will first be looking closely at what needs to be forgiven. This way you will not cover up painful memories by saying they're forgiven without having examined them.

☐ *Choose to stop "cultivating" your bitterness.* In both the Old and New Testament, God uses gardening metaphors when speaking of old anger or bitterness. Hebrews 12:15 speaks of a "bitter root" that causes trouble and "defiles many." It grows up when we miss the full impact of God's grace by *extending* as well as *experiencing* it. And in Psalm 103:9, God is pictured as not "harboring" or "keeping" his anger forever. In the original Hebrew, the term for *harbor* again portrays gardening. "The root [word] is often used in farming contexts of those who keep or guard vineyards."[7] So, God is saying he won't tend the garden of his anger forever. How about you?

After you have taken plenty of time to face the hurtful memories and have begun to feel their pain, you need to come to the place of saying, "Enough is enough!" There is a point when we need to say, "I am ready to let go of the hurt and forgive my hurters. I don't want to cultivate my bitterness forever. It defiles me and those close to me."

For some of us, the thick, powerful root of bitterness and unforgiveness has been pushing its way up through our broken lives for years. It will not yield easily. Remember, forgiveness begins with a choice, but it requires constant recommitment to that choice.

☐ *Study and read about forgiveness to correct any misunderstandings.* A Bible study on forgiveness would be extremely helpful here. In addition, there are several fine books on the topic written by Christian authors.[8]

☐ *Choose to learn about your parents.* Sometimes, when your parents have hurt you deeply, you need to talk to people who knew them when they were young. This will help you understand your parents more fully. If possible, get photographs of your parents when they were children, adolescents and/or young adults. All of this will increase your understanding of your parents and of the forces that shaped their lives and choices. Remember, they are still responsible for their choices, but seeing that your parents are/were weak and needy people just like you will help you forgive them.

☐ *Be specific about the hurts and about forgiving them.* Begin listing specific times your parents or others hurt you. Include the act, your feelings and thoughts at the time, and a space to indicate the date when you chose to forgive. Figure 12-1 is an example from one adult child's list.

Sample Forgiveness List

Hurtful Act	*My Thoughts/Feelings*	*Date Forgiven*
1. Mom called me stupid and clumsy in front of two friends when I was nine.	I wanted to die. I felt so ashamed and humiliated. I thought I must really be a worthless person.	9/21/89
2. My uncle trapped me in a corner at Grandma's on Christmas when I was twelve and he rubbed up against me real hard and French-kissed me.	I felt so dirty and ashamed. I always wondered why he picked me to do that to. I thought maybe he knew something about me that I didn't know myself.	10/7/89

Figure 12-1.

With your list in hand, pour out your feelings and thoughts about the hurtful memory. You can do this by writing a letter you later burn. Or you may want to symbolically seat your hurter in an empty chair in front of you as you do this. After describing each act and expressing your emotions, state aloud or in writing your sincere desire to forgive and release the person(s) who hurt you. It is important to record the date you chose to begin forgiving because you can refer to it when the inevitable emotional setbacks come.

☐ *Choose to forsake your fantasy and grieve the death of "idealized parents."* Most of us have worked our entire lives to earn the "Parental Seal of Approval." Perhaps you have dreamed of having your parents' unconditional love and a close, mutually respectful relationship with them. Forgiving your parents includes forsaking this fantasy and choosing the painful path of grieving the death of that dream of idealized parents.

Let the dream die, grieve and move on with more realistic and respectful expectations and relationships with your parents. As we forsake our fantasies of having perfect parents, and as we grieve the deaths of this dream, we will be more able to forgive our parents for what they did (or didn't do) and accept them for who they are. In so doing, we free ourselves from the bondage of bitterness.

Personal Reflection

☐ Are you willing to begin a "Forgiveness List"? If so, when? If not, why not? What would it take to make you willing?

☐ Are you willing to learn more about your parents? If so, how will you start?

☐ If you can't talk with your parents, with whom could you talk to get more information about them? When will you do this?

☐ If you are not now willing to learn more about your parents, why not? What would help you be willing?

☐ Are you punishing yourself for any past, forsaken sin? If so, get your Bible, and read 1 John 1:7-9. What does God say about your sin if you have confessed it and turned from it?

☐ Write a brief prayer thanking God for purifying you from all sin by the blood of Christ.

☐ If you are willing, write a brief prayer asking God to empower you to forgive others just as he has forgiven you.

Looking Ahead

I confess I held out on you before. There is one final forgiveness principle from Joseph's story. In Genesis 50:20, we see that forgiveness also includes *a redemptive perspective.*

"You intended to harm me, *but God intended it for good to accomplish what is now being done,* the saving of many lives." (Genesis 50:20, emphasis added.)

In this one verse, we see that Joseph had both a realistic view of the past and a redemptive perspective on the future. Joseph had experienced what it meant to be released for potential and purpose. And so can you.

13
Released for Potential and Purpose

*A*s *Christian adult children, we may wonder what our potentials are* as weak and broken people. And what purposes are being served by all our struggles and pain? These are fair questions. Fortunately, the Bible talks about potential and purpose in ways that encourage us.

The Potential of Weakness

God uses weak and needy people because these are the only kind he has. He never promises to eliminate our weaknesses. Instead, God promises that, "the [Holy] Spirit helps us in our weakness. . . . (see Romans 8:26).

Have you seen the photograph of a straw that was driven into a telephone pole during a tornado? The potential for that amazing act was not in the weakness of the straw but in the power of the tornado. That photo pictures precisely the central issue in the question of potential. The potential for transforming our weaknesses lies not in us but in God's unlimited power.

I heard an interesting story about the city fathers of New York. Years ago as they laid out the streets, numbering from the center outward, they projected how large the city would grow. At the time there were only six or seven streets, so—letting their imaginations run wild, they drew the map all the way out to 19th Street. In fact, they called it "Boundard Street." From our present perspective, we would call them a bit shortsighted since, at last count, New York City had grown to 285th Street.

We often behave the way those city planners did. With our limited imaginations we think we're dreaming big, but in reality we're failing to see God's potential for transforming our lives. Right now you might be saying, "Don't call it 'limited imagination.' You don't know the degradation and despair in my background."

If you're saying that, I'm not surprised. I have felt that way, and most of my clients have felt that way as well. One client, Pauline, may voice your feelings.

"My entire life has been one mistake after another. I really mean it. I feel like a walking, talking error," Pauline declared.

An unwanted, unloved child in a violently dysfunctional family, Pauline's adult life was characterized by repeated, abusive relationships. And she was morbidly obese because she spent years overeating to self-medicate her emotional pain. Pauline is now a new Christian struggling to believe in God's potential to transform her life. She has no trouble accepting the truth of Ephesians 2:8-9, that God's gift of grace brought her salvation. But she cannot grasp the Ephesians 2:10 picture of herself as God's masterpiece. And yet, she is!

From a Mistake to a Masterpiece

What Pauline has a hard time understanding is that a true master can transform *anything* into a masterpiece. I once heard about a group of English fishermen who went into a village inn at the close of a long day. After ordering tea, they began recounting the day's adventures. As one particularly exuberant fisherman threw out his arms to illustrate the size of his best catch, he accidentally hit the pot of tea being brought to their table. Dark liquid splashed against the clean, white-washed wall of the inn, forming a large, ugly stain.

Naturally, the fisherman was aghast and apologetic. Just then, a man seated at a nearby table approached and told the fisherman to calm himself. The stranger removed a pen from his jacket and began to draw on the wall. In moments, he created the head of a beautiful stag, transforming the embarrassing stain into majestic antlers. Bystanders could hardly believe their eyes. Only a few recognized the artist as Sir Edwin Landseer, England's foremost painter of wildlife. What had been a disfiguring, ugly stain became the inn's most prized possession. People came from miles around to admire Landseer's handiwork.

Time Out

It doesn't matter how dark the stains are in your life. God's creative potential is unlimited. He can take the very thing you view as most hideous and transform it into something that will make you most useable to him.

But it doesn't happen automatically; you must invite God into your life to do it. Please read the following verses until they have a chance to sink in:

> For it is by grace you have been saved, through faith—and this not from yourselves, it is the gift of God—not by works, so that no one can boast. For we are God's workmanship, created in Christ Jesus to do good works, which God prepared in advance for us to do. (Ephesians 2:8-10)

These verses assure us that God's transforming power is part of a "package deal." God does not begin to make you his workmanship or masterpiece until you have become his child by receiving his gift of grace by faith.

☐ If you have never done that, would you do it now?

☐ If you have already acted on the truth of verses 8 and 9, would you ask God to give you the faith to move into the truth of verse 10?

The Purpose of Brokenness

Like Pauline, you may see your life as the sum of countless mistakes—yours or others—that have left you bruised and broken. But God's commitment to our redemption means he desires to transform the dysfunctional traits of adult children into useful qualities. For example, in God's hands that sense of our incompleteness that drives us to self-help sections of bookstores can be transformed into a teachable spirit.

When God transforms us, God demonstrates that he never wastes the pain of his children. God the Father did not waste the pain and suffering of his own Son, but used it redemptively to purchase our salvation. Of course, our personal pain doesn't pay anyone's sin debt, but God's redemptive purposes can be served in our lives in at least three ways.

☐ *Living through pain can help us develop character.* My goal for my life is to be "healthy, wealthy and wise"—and hassle-free. *God's* goal for my life is that I be more and more conformed to the image of his Son by developing a Christlike character. And he uses the painful trials and struggles of living in a sinful world to accomplish his purpose. Chuck Swindoll has suggested that a pearl perfectly illustrates this.

Pearls are the product of pain. For some unknown reason, the shell of the oyster gets pierced and an alien substance—a grain of sand—slips inside. On the entry of that foreign irritant, all the resources within the tiny, sensitive oyster rush to the spot and begin to release healing fluids that otherwise would have remained dormant. By and by the irritant is covered and the wound is healed—by a *pearl.* No other gem has so fascinating a history. It is the symbol of stress—a healed wound . . . a precious, tiny jewel conceived through irritation, born of adversity, nursed by adjustments. Had there been no wounding, no irritating interruption, there could have been no pearl.[1]

In James 1:2-4, God tells us to welcome "trials" as friends, not enemies, because they develop mature, Christlike character in believers. Your response to that truth may be a little like the child who had a tonsillectomy. She was frightened of the surgery, so her folks promised to give her the kitten she'd been wanting for so long. The surgery went well, but as the anesthesia was wearing off, the little girl was heard muttering to herself, "What a lousy way to get a cat!"

Living with trials and suffering seems like a lousy way to develop Christlike character. Frankly, I would prefer that God used uninterrupted bliss for the same purpose. However, in this fallen world filled with sin-broken people making sin-shaped choices, uninterrupted bliss is in very short supply. Meanwhile, there are an abundance of trials and suffering. This painful reality relates to another of God's purposes for broken people.

☐ *Living through pain gives us the resources to comfort others.* In a world where sinful human beings are free to make sinful choices, there will always be a lot of people needing a lot of comfort. Who better for the job than those who have suffered and have sought and found comfort in God? This is the message of 2 Corinthians 1:3-4.

Praise be to the God and Father of our Lord Jesus Christ, the Father of compassion and God of all comfort, who comforts us in all our troubles, so that we can comfort those in any trouble with the comfort we ourselves have received from God.

As we continue in our recovering processes, experiencing more and more of God's love, forgiveness and comfort, we will become effective agents of God's comfort in the lives of others. This process includes encouraging others to find their ultimate comfort in God as we tell them about how he comforted us.

☐ *Living through pain gives us a way to glorify God.* The highest purpose for all of life, including the stewardship of suffering, is to bring glory to our creator/redeemer God. One of the most dramatic pictures of this is found in Psalm 107 where the "redeemed of the Lord" are repeatedly exhorted to bring God glory by telling others about the marvelous ways in which he has rescued them.

On April 3, 1988, Garth and I celebrated our thirtieth wedding anniversary. Part of what made that day so special was that our entire church—packed beyond capacity for Easter morning—acknowledged our joy with a prayer of blessing during the service, and warm words and greetings after.

But I didn't want the congregation to think that Garth and I had giggled our way through thirty idyllic years of "perfect marriage." And I didn't want to miss a chance to glorify God for the healing he had brought in us and in our marriage.

The next week it was my turn to write an article for the church newsletter. I wrote about how our marriage was a triumph of God's grace in the lives of two selfish, broken sinners. I wanted the congregation to know that God had worked a miracle in both of us, and that we both knew it and praised him for it. It felt wonderful to encourage others who might be going through hard times. But my greatest joy was having the chance to glorify God for his lovingkindness to me.

Now, you might think you've messed up too much to begin trying to give God glory and offer hope to others. If so, consider the apostle Paul's situation described in Acts 27:21-25. While Paul is being transported to Rome to stand trial, his ship is caught in a storm that will result in a shipwreck. In the midst of the storm, Paul gives God glory and assures everyone of God's promise that they reach shore alive. Don't you think Paul might have wondered if anyone would take him and his mighty God seriously? After all, Paul's mighty God hadn't even set him free! We'll never know what Paul was thinking, but we do know that he glorified God in the midst of his less-than-perfect circumstances.

If I put off glorifying God until every aspect of my life felt and looked "redeemed" and in order, I would never do it—neither would you. Begin where you are. Begin now.

Looking Ahead

I've been told that effective communication contains three components: *what? so what?* and *now what?* The first twelve chapters have been the "what" part of this book. This chapter thus far has articulated my "so what." section. The third component, *now what?* begins when you close the book.

The real work comes now, when you stop *reading* about new choices for change and you start *practicing* them. Two commitments are essential:

☐ *You must commit yourself to continually learning the truth.* By now you know I think our feelings are very important. But you can vent your feelings forever and no real healing will occur without changing your shame-based thinking. You must continue to learn the truth of God to replace the shame-based lies that have caused you to stumble. Psalm 119:165 promises "Great peace have they who love [God's Word], and nothing can make them stumble."

☐ *You must commit yourself to consistently practicing the truth.* Learning truth is necessary but not sufficient to bring change. If you just put this book down and begin reading another one containing more truth, your life and relationships still won't change. Truth-based change comes from living new, truth-shaped choices. Jesus declared this in John 13:17 when he said, "Now that you know these things, you will be blessed if you do them."

Your recovering process will be different from mine or anyone else's. That's as it should be because you are as unique as your personal history. But there will be similar outcomes: less dependence on others in conformity to the world and more dependence on God in conformity to Christ.

God stands ready to do for you what he is doing for me and for countless other Christian adults raised in dysfunctional families. He is teaching us to live in the freedom of grace and truth. He is breaking the bondage of our pasts and leading us into futures where we are being increasingly released from shame.

Appendix A
Renunciation of Occultic and Satanic Influences

These practices may open our lives to the Enemy by providing a foothold for him (see Ephesians 4:27).

Some Occultic Practices to Renounce:

1. Astral projection
2. Astrology
3. Automatic writing
4. Bio-rhythms (when mixed with stars)
5. Channeling
6. Clairvoyance
7. E.S.P.
8. Fortune telling
9. Horoscopes
10. Kabala
11. Levitation
12. Magic—"black" or "white" (Wicka)
13. Mental telepathy
14. Mind control
15. Mediums
16. Ouija boards
17. Palm reading
18. Pyramids and/or crystals
19. Psychic healing
20. Parapsychology
21. Reincarnation
22. Seances
23. Tarot cards
24. Tea leaf reading
25. Telekinesis
26. Transcendental meditation

Some Occultic and Satanic Religions to Renounce:

1. Buddhism	7. Scientology
2. Christian Science	8. Temple of Set
3. Church of Satan	9. Unity
4. Hinduism	10. Voodoo
5. Krishna	11. Wicka
6. Moon	12. Yoga

Some Other Occultic and/or Satanic Influences to Renounce:
1. Dungeons & Dragons "game"
2. Drug use (especially hallucinogenic)
3. Heavy-metal music, for instance, Slayer

Some Sinful Attitudes and Practices to Renounce:
1. "Old" anger or rage/resentment/bitterness/unforgiveness (see Ephesians 4:26-27)
2. Rebellion/persistent pride and disobedience (see 1 Samuel 15:23)

Prayer of Renunciation (From *The Adversary* by Mark I. Bubeck)
Blessed Heavenly Father, I ask your forgiveness for offending you by committing this sin of (name the offense). I claim the cleansing that is mine through the blood of the Lord Jesus Christ. I address myself against Satan and all his kingdom. I take away from you and all your powers of darkness any ground you are claiming against me when I sinned in (name the offense). I claim that ground back in the name of the Lord Jesus Christ. I cover it with the blood of the Lord Jesus Christ and give all areas of my life over to the full control of the Holy Spirit.

Appendix B
Your Identity in Christ

The following Scripture passages will help get you started seeing yourself as God sees you.

1. *John 1:12; 1 Peter 2:9*—(You are a child of God, and you belong to him.)

2. *Romans 8:35-39*—(You are loved by God, and nothing can separate you from his love.)

3. *Ephesians 1:4*—(You are chosen by God.)

4. *John 17:9, 12, 14*—(You are a gift to Jesus from God.)

5. *Romans 8:28, 30*—(You have been called by God.)

6. *John 17:9; Hebrews 7:25*—(You are in Jesus' prayers.)

7. *Ephesians 2:18; 3:12*—(You have access to God through Jesus.)

8. *Colossians 2:13-14*—(You are forgiven and your sin debt is paid.)

9. *Romans 8:1*—(You are not condemned.)

10. *Philippians 4:13*—(You are strengthened for all tasks to which God calls you.)

11. *Ephesians 2:10; Philippians 1:6; 2:13*—(You are God's handiwork.)

12. *1 Corinthians 6:19; John 14:16*—(Your body is the Holy Spirit's abode.)

13. *John 6:47*—(You have everlasting life.)

14. *John 10:10*—(You have abundant life.)

15. *Romans 5:1*—(You have peace with God through the Lord Jesus Christ.)

16. *Philippians 4:7*—(You have the peace of God which transcends understanding.)

17. *Colossians 1:13*—(You have been rescued from the dominion of darkness and brought into the kingdom of God's Son.)

18. *Philippians 4:19*—(You have all your needs met according to God's glorious riches in Christ Jesus.)

Appendix C
Attributes of God

1. *God is compassionate* as demonstrated in his mercy and loving-kindness. "The LORD is compassionate and gracious, slow to anger, abounding in love" (Psalm 103:8).

2. *God is forgiving* because of his grace and mercy. Jesus paid our sin debts so that God could forgive sin while remaining holy and just. "In him [Christ] we have redemption through his blood, the forgiveness of sins, in accordance with the riches of God's grace" (Ephesians 1:7). See also Romans 3:23-26.

3. *God is holy* because of his absolute moral excellence. "For the Mighty One has done great things for me—holy is his name" (Luke 1:49).

4. *God is immutable,* that is to say, he never changes. "Jesus Christ is the same yesterday and today and forever" (Hebrews 13:8).

5. *God is just* because he always acts fairly, in accordance with his nature. "He is the Rock, his works are perfect, and all his ways are just. A faithful God who does no wrong, upright and just is he" (Deuteronomy 32:4).

6. *God is loving* because of his nature and not because of anything we do to elicit his love. His love is expressed in actions toward us. "God is love" (1 John 4:16).

7. *God is omnipotent* because he has unlimited power and ability. "You have made the heavens and the earth by your great power and outstretched arm.

Nothing is too hard for you" (Jeremiah 32:17).

8. *God is omnipresent* because he is present everywhere in the universe at the same time. He is never "absent." " 'Am I only a God nearby,' declares the LORD, 'and not a God far away? Can anyone hide in secret places so that I cannot see him?' declares the LORD. 'Do not I fill heaven and earth?' declares the LORD" (Jeremiah 23:23-24.)

9. *God is omniscient* because of his unlimited knowledge and wisdom. "You know when I sit and when I rise; you perceive my thoughts from afar. You discern my going out and my lying down; you are familiar with all my ways. Before a word is on my tongue you know it completely, O LORD" (Psalm 139:2-4).

10. *God is righteous* because he only does what is right and is free from any wrongdoing. "The LORD is righteous in all his ways and loving toward all he has made" (Psalm 145:17).

11. *God is sovereign* because he rules supremely over all creation. "He does as he pleases with the powers of heaven and the peoples of the earth. No one can hold back his hand or say to him: 'What have you done?' " (Daniel 4:35).

12. *God is truthful* because, in accordance with his nature, he cannot lie. "For the faith of God's elect and the knowledge of the truth . . . leads to godliness— a faith and knowledge resting on the hope of eternal life, which God, who does not lie, promised before the beginning of time" (Titus 1:1-2).

Notes

Chapter 1: My Story: "Half a Loaf"
[1]Sandra Wilson, "Evangelical Christian Adult Children of Alcoholics: A Preliminary Study," *The Journal of Psychology and Theology* 17 (1989), pp. 263-73. Sandra Wilson, *Counseling Adult Children of Alcoholics*, Resources for Christian Counseling, vol. 21, ed. Gary Collins (Dallas: Word Books, 1989), p. 145.

[2]Recently, mental health professionals have begun to examine the effects of "father loss" and "father hunger" on children from dysfunctional and divorced families. Their consensus is that "a mother, no matter how competent, can't offer male approval." This has profoundly negative influences on a daughter's self-esteem and relationships with men. (Carol Lacey, "Unwary Fathers Hinder Daughters' Success," *The Cincinnati Enquirer*, July 30, 1989, p. E-8.)

Chapter 2: Understanding Shame and Stumbling
[1]Gershen Kaufman, *Shame* (Rochester, Vt.: Schenkman Books, 1985), pp. 8-13.

[2]I agree with those who say that we also experience shame from *cultural* sources. Nevertheless, I believe a child's early family environment determines the extent to which he or she will be influenced by cultural sources of binding shame.

[3]Walter Bauer, William F. Arndt and F. Wilbur Gingrich, *A Greek-English Lexicon of the New Testament* 2nd ed. (Chicago: University of Chicago Press, 1979), p. 752.

[4]Barbara Wood, *Children of Alcoholism: The Struggle for Self and Intimacy in Adult Life* (New York: University Press, 1987), p. 23.

Chapter 4: Rules in Dysfunctional Families
[1]"Boys on Death Row: More Mad Than Bad?" *Harvard Medical School Mental*

Health Letter 3 (1988), p. 6. Emphasis not in the original.
[2]Rokelle Lerner, *Boundaries for Codependents* (Center City, Minn.: Hazelden, 1988), p. 13.
[3]In my research with 129 evangelical Christians, I found that those from one type of dysfunctional family (alcoholic) were significantly more distrusting of God and others than the subjects from nonalcoholic homes. (I am using "significantly" in the sense of statistical significance.) For details, see Sandra Wilson, "Evangelical Christian Adult Children of Alcoholics: A Preliminary Study," *The Journal of Psychology and Theology* 17 (1989), pp. 263-73.

Chapter 5: Abuse and Shaming in Dysfunctional Families
[1]Paul Clancy, "Child Sex Abuse: 'Crime of the '90s' " *USA Today,* September 29, 1989, p. A-3. Emphasis not in the original.
[2]Stephen Rothman, "Heart of Darkness," *Changes,* June 1990, pp. 34-36, 59-63.
[3]Kathleen Parker, "Divorce Gives Some Children 'Father Hunger,' " *The Cincinnati Enquirer,* June 25, 1989, p. E-2.

Chapter 6: Abuse and Shaming by Christian Parents
[1]Grant Martin, *Counseling for Family Violence and Abuse,* Resources for Christian Counseling, vol. 6, ed. Gary Collins (Dallas: Word Books, 1987), p. 149.
[2]Carmen Berrty, *When Helping You Is Hurting Me: Escaping the Messiah Trap* (San Francisco: Harper & Row, 1988), p. 6.
[3]Ibid., p. 16.
[4]Francis Brown, S. R. Driver and Charles Briggs, *A Hebrew and English Lexicon of the Old Testament* (Oxford: Clarendon Press, 1968), p. 457.

Chapter 7: Understanding Consequences and Change
[1]Bill Keller, "Soviets Admit Public Maps Phoney," *The Cincinnati Enquirer,* September 3, 1988, p. A-1.
[2]Earnie Larsen, *What I Practice, I Become* (St. Paul, Minn.: International Marriage Encounter, 1986), p. 17.
[3]David Seamands, *Healing for Damaged Emotions* (Wheaton, Ill.: Victor Books, 1982), p. 23.

Chapter 8: Released from Shaming Our Flaws
[1]You may think I am exaggerating to say that unwillingness to acknowledge physical limitations could lead to death. The last days of Muppet originator Jim Henson suggest otherwise. *People* magazine (June 18, 1990, pp. 88-96)

reported that Henson's death at age 53 was caused not just by the severe but treatable disease he had but by "his own character." "Henson's . . . desire never to bother anyone became a genuinely tragic flaw in the end. Not wanting to trouble his family, not wanting to trouble the doctors—these were the reasons he postponed going to the hospital until it was six to eight hours too late." It appears that Henson was embarrassed and ashamed to be ill enough to need help. This attitude may appear humble, but it can also be lethal.
[2]Anita Bechel, "Our Bodies . . . Temples of the Holy Spirit," *The Evangelical Beacon*, January 29, 1990, p. 4.
[3]Keith Sehert, *Selfcare Wellcare* (Minneapolis, Minn.: Augsburg, 1985), p. 17.

Chapter 9: Released from Shaming Our Feelings
[1]See Luke 10:21, where Jesus "rejoiced greatly" at the good report of the seventy he had sent out to announce the kingdom of God. See also John 11:35, where Christ wept at Lazarus's grave, and Matthew 26:38, where he "deeply grieved" in Gethsemane. In John 2:14-16, we see Jesus angry and responding appropriately to this emotion.
[2]Recent research indicates that even a "single instance of overwhelming terror can alter the chemistry of the brain, making people more sensitive to adrenalin surges [which are] major factors in post-traumatic stress disorder, in which people can experience normal events as repetitions of the original trauma. . . . The more intense the trauma, and the longer it lasts, the more likely it is to result in post-traumatic stress." See Daniel Goleman, "Terror May Alter Brain for Life, Study Says," *The Cincinnati Enquirer*, June 12, 1990, pp. A-1, A-12.
[3]For example, see Exodus 22:22-24, Deuteronomy 29:18-21 and Joshua 7:1.
[4]Norma Peterson, "Daily Hassles May Be a Health Hazard," *USA Today*, March 30, 1988, p. D-3. Emphasis not in the original.
[5]Bob Sipchen, "The Powerful Pursuit of Intoxication," *The Cincinnati Enquirer*, August 27, 1989, p. E-5.
[6]Jim Knippenberg, "Tipoff: Ice Cream Habits," *The Cincinnati Enquirer*, September 20, 1989, p. E-1.
[7]Many religious leaders and some mental health professionals object to using the term *addiction* to describe behaviors such as habitual sexual promiscuity. However, there is some evidence showing that sexual arousal triggers an increase in the release of mood-altering chemical messengers in the brain. "It is possible that sex addicts try to get the high that results from those chemicals." See Barbara Dolan, "Do People Get Hooked on Sex?" *Time*, June 4, 1990, p. 72.

[8]Craig Nakken, *The Addictive Personality* (Center City, Minn.: Hazelden, 1988), p. 17.

[9]For example, see Proverbs 23:7, Mark 7:20, Matthew 15:18-19, and Romans 12:2.

[10]Sandra Wilson, *Counseling Adult Children of Alcoholics,* Resources for Christian Counseling, vol. 21, ed. Gary Collins (Dallas: Word Books, 1989), p. 145.

Chapter 10: Released from Shame-based Codependency
[1]Melody Beattie, *Beyond Codependency* (San Francisco: Harper/Hazelden, 1989), p. 153.

[2]Ronald Potter-Efron and Patricia Potter-Efron, *I Deserve Respect: Finding and Healing Shame in Personal Relationships* (Center City, Minn.: Hazelden, 1989), p. 3.

[3]Several of the following suggested choices are adapted from Sandra Wilson, *Counseling Adult Children of Alcoholics,* Resources for Christian Counseling, vol. 21, ed. Gary Collins (Dallas: Word Books, 1989), pp. 186-190.

[4]Herbert L. Gravitz and Julie D. Bowden, *Guide to Recovery: A Book for Adult Children of Alcoholics* (Holmes Beach, Fla.: Learning Publications, 1985), p. 73.

[5]Krista Ramsey, "Two-Parent Family Soon a Minority," *The Cincinnati Enquirer,* October 14, 1989, p. A-1.

Chapter 11: Released from Shame-based Concepts of God and Religion
[1]Herbert Vanderlugt, "Unrealized Blessings, *Our Daily Bread* (Grand Rapids, MI: Radio Bible Class), November 23, 1988.

[2]The concept of "distorted deities" is developed more fully in my book *Counseling Adult Children of Alcoholics,* Resources for Christian Counseling, vol. 21, ed. Gary Collins (Dallas: Word Books, 1989), pp. 95-100.

[3]My research with Christian adult children of alcoholics demonstrated statistically that they had much more difficulty trusting God and experiencing his love and forgiveness than Christians from nonalcoholic families. For details, see Wilson, "Evangelical Christian Adult Children of Alcoholics: A Preliminary Study," *The Journal of Psychology and Theology* 17 (1989), pp. 263-73.

[4]Figure 11-1 is loosely adapted from Margaret Rinck, *Can Christians Love Too Much?* (Grand Rapids, Mich.: Zondervan, 1989), p. 154.

[5]Walter Bauer, William F. Arndt and F. Wilbur Gingrich, *A Greek-English Lexicon of the New Testament,* 2nd ed. (Chicago: University of Chicago Press, 1979), p. 81.

[6]Mark DeHaan, "Why Shoot Our Wounded?, *Our Daily Bread* (Grand Rapids, Mich.: Radio Bible Class), December 10, 1989.

[7]Many of the following suggestions are adapted from my book *Counseling Adult Children of Alcoholics*, pp. 241-44.

[8]For example, see Warren Myers and Ruth Myers, *Experiencing God's Attributes* (Colorado Springs, Colo.: NavPress, 1978).

[9]Robert McGee, *The Search for Significance* (Houston: Rapha, 1987), p. 82.

[10]Philip Yancey, "Saturday Seven Days a Week," *Christianity Today*, March 18, 1988, p. 64.

Chapter 12: Released to Forgive the Shamers

[1]Terry Lawhead, " 'Toxic Parents' Can Poison Children," *The Cincinnati Enquirer*, August 18, 1989, p. B-10.

[2]Gayle Rosellini and Mark Worden, *Taming Your Turbulent Past* (Pompano Beach, Fla.: Health Communications, 1987), p. 179.

[3]Sandra Wilson, *Counseling Adult Children of Alcoholics*, Resources for Christian Counseling, vol. 21, ed. Gary Collins (Dallas: Word Books, 1989), p. 259.

[4]Arnold Fox and Barry Fox, "The Gift of Forgiveness: Giving up the Emotional Toxins," *Changes*, May-June 1989, p. 18.

[5]Walter Bauer, William F. Arndt and F. Wilbur Gingrich, *A Greek-English Lexicon of the New Testament*, 2nd ed., Chicago: University of Chicago Press, p. 125.

[6]W. E. Vine, *An Expository Dictionary of New Testament Words* (Old Tappan, N.J.: Fleming H. Revell, 1966), p. 224.

[7]R. Laird Harris, Gleason Archer and Bruce Weltke, *Theological Word Book of the Old Testament*, vol. 2 (Chicago: Moody Press, 1980), p. 576.

[8]A few examples are: Charles Stanley, *Forgiveness* (Nashville, Tenn.: Oliver Nelson, 1987); Lewis Smedes, *Forgive and Forget* (New York: Harper & Row, 1984); and Richard Walters, *Forgive and Be Free* (Grand Rapids, Mich.: Zondervan, 1983).

Chapter 13: Released for Potential and Purpose

[1]Charles Swindoll, *Starting Over* (Portland, Ore.: Multnomah Press, 1977), pp. 40-41.

362.82
W753

82844

LINCOLN CHRISTIAN COLLEGE AND SEMINARY

3 4711 00169 3847